Why Your
CHILDREN
Won't Get To
HEAVEN

R. J. Wenzel

To Mary Wenzel, beloved mother and extraordinary Ember

Why Your Children Won't Get To Heaven

©2020 R. J. Wenzel

print ISBN: 978-1-09833-091-0

CONTENTS

ACKNOWLEDGMENTS

I would like to thank my sister, Jo Jackson, for her enormous role in writing this book. It would not have been possible without her continuous support, and it would be far less comprehensible without her many suggestions and skilled editing.

Many persons also contributed information and suggestions. I am especially grateful to Peggy Muehlemann, Donna Kallal, and Fr. Dominique Bourmaud for their help in researching historical events.

Endless thanks to my wife, Diane and son, Ben for their suggestions and for their patient support of this project from the beginning.

And of course, the book would not even have been conceived without my mother, Mary. Her years of reading and writing (and saving carbon copies) resulted in a trove of documents that aided research immeasurably. Her keen memory helped connect dots that would otherwise never have been obvious.

And her positive outlook continually energized the effort.

PREFACE

For years now, I've spent an afternoon or two every week with my mother at her kitchen table, just talking. We discuss and debate endless subjects, though we're mostly drawn to favorites like baseball, politics, current events, kids, grandkids, world affairs, religion. First let it be known that the reason we can immerse ourselves in almost any topic is: Mom is well-versed in almost any topic. She's moving a bit slower now at ninety years of age, but hasn't lost a step upstairs. As far as I can tell, she remembers just about everything she's seen, done, or learned over those nine decades and is glad to share it all, along with as much cogent analysis as the occasion requires. Our conversations are really more like brainstorming sessions, peppered with new information, always in search of logical explanations for what the heck is going on.

In recent years our conversations tend toward religion more than other topics. That is mostly my doing, since I'm at a phase in life where faith is becoming more important. Then again, when talking Church, we seldom get far without crossing into politics and current events, sometimes even other areas. We are a Roman Catholic family in the year 2020. Religion is, well, complicated.

One of our favorite topics has always been the struggle that tradition-minded "Latin Mass" Catholics (like Mom) have endured since the Second Vatican Council of the 1960's. On this topic she has an endless supply of stories, often backed up with photos or documents from her experience. Our discussions have helped me understand how the Catholic Church transformed itself quickly after Vatican II and have also given me a feel for what Catholicism was like before the 1960's. I've actually found it all very interesting, which is surprising since I'd never been particularly curious about Church history.

Very much connected to her understanding of and belief in the Catholic faith, my mother has long been haunted by one problem. She has 6 living children, 19 grandchildren, and 18 great grandchildren and they are not all practicing Catholics. If they do not know and practice the faith, how will those family members make it to heaven? And second only to mother's desire to get to heaven herself, is a desire for her family to be there with her. If my mother is troubled by the children/grandchildren dilemma, I would wager that countless other Catholic parents feel the same way.

As luck would have it, the "children dilemma" combined with our previous exploration into the Tradition of the Church turned out to be very relevant when in 2018, a tide of bizarre happenings in the Catholic Church (scandals, confusion over moral teachings, etc.) began dominating our discussions. We tried to figure out what - if anything – these situations should mean to us ordinary Catholics, and maybe even what we should do about them. Wide-ranging conversations led us to some very useful conclusions, but something interesting and even more consequential happened along the way. We found that we only made real progress in understanding what was going on in the Church today when we factored in information about Church history and Catholic Tradition. That realization eventually led to this book.

Church history and Catholic Tradition, or more appropriately how Tradition has been jettisoned and systematically denied to Catholics for many decades, can help us understand why so many Catholics at this unique point in history might not be on a path to Heaven. And understanding this puts us in a position to take action. This book is written to help you change perspective and move forward, as if you too had been at our kitchen table. Read it. Share it. It is never too late for your children to get to Heaven, until it is!

INTRODUCTION

You are in heaven, peering out through the pearly gates as Johnny walks away. All those years on earth, but he never quite managed to figure out what God meant by a "good and faithful servant." And yes, it is too late now. You knew your kid wasn't a sure thing for Heaven, but you hoped anyway. You prayed for him. Yet there you stand watching as he is sent away, a knot in your stomach, thinking "If only I'd done more."

Today, in real time, Johnny is a "nominal" Catholic. He may or may not be going through the motions. Either way, he hardly seems a sure bet for Heaven. Let us acknowledge of course that none of us actually knows the threshold requirements for getting to Heaven. Still I bet we can all at least agree on signs that Johnny (or Suzie) appears to be taking unnecessary risks with attaining eternal salvation. Further, we would probably agree that few thinking Catholics would *knowingly* take unnecessary risks – considering the stakes. What Johnny needs now is someone to help him *know* the risk.

How do any of us understand the risks our children may be taking with their eternal souls? Are we even taking some risks ourselves? Since the extent to which we recognize risks depends on how well we see the "whole picture," the vast majority of Catholics today could have reason to be very concerned. We have trouble seeing the danger we are in personally because the whole picture is not in front of us. There is a missing piece: Sacred Tradition.[1] And

---

1 The Catechism of the Catholic Church (CCC) describes Tradition as the living transmission of apostolic preaching, guided by the Holy Spirit and preserved in a continuous line of succession from the apostles through their successors. "Through Tradition, the Church, in her doctrine, life, and worship, perpetuates and transmits to every generation, all that she herself is, all that she believes."

there is a reason for this: it has been kept from us - for the last sixty years.[2] The purpose of this book is to help today's Catholic (especially parents and grandparents) rediscover Sacred Tradition and to recognize the vital role it must play in helping our families survive these difficult times and achieve our ultimate purpose.

It took years for me, an ordinary Catholic, to begin seeing the importance of Catholic Tradition. For as long as I can remember, I thought of Catholic Tradition like any other "tradition": customs we had developed and continued, but not exactly consequential in the whole scheme of things. Since those customs were relatively unimportant, I had no reason to question them, but I wouldn't question changes to them either. Then at some point I stumbled onto the Deposit of the Faith, and its meaning.[3] Sacred Tradition, I (re)learned, is one of three indispensable components of the Deposit of the Faith (along with Sacred Scripture and Magisterium), even predating the other two (starting the moment the Church was formed at Pentecost). But still, the enormous importance of Sacred Catholic Tradition was slow to sink in. Thankfully, over time, it did. This quote from the Catechism of the Catholic Church speaks volumes:

> *"Both Scripture and Tradition must be accepted and honored with equal sentiments of devotion and reverence."*

Wow. So Sacred Tradition is hugely important.[4] Got it.

---

2 This book will not explore why the Catholic Church has suppressed Tradition. While this is an important question, proper treatment would be lengthy and take us too far from our intended focus. The reader is wholeheartedly encouraged to pursue the question. Helpful information is included in the Appendix.

3 The "Sacred Deposit" of the faith consists of **Sacred Scripture + Tradition.** Bishops, working with the Pope, are responsible for authentic interpretation of the Sacred Deposit over time, which is called the **Magisterium.** Together these three are considered the whole teaching of the Faith, sometimes collectively referred to as the **Deposit of the Faith.**

4 For a Catholic, trying to understand our Faith without Tradition is like trying to sit on two-legged stool.

That makes the claim above (that Tradition has been kept from us for the last sixty years), if true, something that would be a really big deal. It is. I would not have believed it if I hadn't learned the details of what has happened in the years between 1960 and today. And I don't blame other Catholics for doubting it, either. That is the reason parts one through three of this book are dedicated to the events of that period. This is something we ordinary Catholics must come to grips with, and it takes time to soak in. To this end, these chapters attempt to help you travel a path similar to mine – but more quickly. Be advised it will not be a scholarly dive into Sacred Catholic Tradition. Not at all! Rather, it is a quick immersion into the last fifty years in the Catholic Church via the experiences of real Catholics in the pew as the Church changed from what it was before Vatican II - to what it is today. The focus is on *Embers*: individual persons, burning with traditional Catholic faith, passionate about sacred practices that existed before Vatican II. They would not give up their beloved traditional practices and beliefs, and consequently they lived the events of the last fifty years in a different way than most Catholics. In getting to know the stories of Embers, it also becomes clear that today's traditional movement in the Church isn't a sudden phenomenon. There is actually nothing new at all about it.

From the Ember stories you will surely gain insight into *how* the Church pulled off its transformation. And you will pick up bits of actual Catholic Tradition that may be useful going forward. But the biggest payoff will be your informed conviction that the vast majority of today's Catholics (Johnny included) are showing up to a gun fight with only a knife in hand. Almost all Catholics under the age of sixty five have lived their lives in a Church that has actively worked to suppress the *full* Deposit of the Faith, most notably Sacred Tradition. The absence of Tradition blinds us from seeing and understanding what is happening in the Church today and our place in it, from recognizing the risks we are taking.

Armed with a new understanding of the importance and role of Catholic Tradition, we are able to move into Part Four and address the two important questions of this book:

1. Why Johnny (or Suzie) won't get to heaven

2. Whether you can alter that future, setting course for a family reunion in eternity

Make no mistake, serious obstacles are in front of Johnny. And because his rightful inheritance (the full Deposit of the Faith) was denied him, he doesn't even have the tools needed to understand and overcome them. A family reunion in heaven depends on us helping Johnny claw back his rightful inheritance, put things in perspective, and make bold decisions going forward. A tall order indeed, but within reach if we seize the initiative.

PART ONE:
WINDS OF CHANGE ARRIVE ON MAIN STREET

*The Modernist storm crashes into Churches everywhere
… battering the lives of orthodox Catholics*

CHAPTER 1:
BACK WHEN...

BACK WHEN SISTER TAUGHT SCHOOL

Times were pretty good in July of 1929 as a middle class family on the North side of St. Louis welcomed their first-born, Mary, into the world. Before long, however, this young family would be shaken by the great economic crash. Two tough years passed before Dad landed a steady job at a stove foundry across the river in Illinois. The young family packed their bags for the small community of Belleville, and moved into the first of three of homes they would occupy over the next 60 years. For the record, all of those homes would be within the boundaries of St. Mary's Catholic Parish.

Through her childhood years, Mary dutifully walked every day to St. Mary's Grade School. Girls in plaid skirts and white blouses, boys in navy pants and white shirts, all streamed into the building and darted to their classrooms. At first bell came the all-school march across the courtyard to morning Mass, with one of the girls digging for a tissue, to substitute for her forgotten chapel veil. Once in church, the students filed down the center aisle past elder parishioners seated in the back of church. The elders observed the parade, then re-focused back into their missals as the weekday Mass started. Forty five minutes later classes were in session back across the courtyard. Sister Aurelia, her face peering out from the full habit of the School Sisters of Notre Dame, spoke softly as she steered class through math, reading, English, and religion. She rarely needed to discipline, but dished it out quickly when called for. The daily class schedule was routine. Periodically through the week, though, Father Joseph Orlet knocked at the door and strolled under the transom, unmistakable in his full black cassock.

The pastor would remove his three-peaked black biretta, set it gently on the stool beneath the crucifix and the U.S. flag, and then proceed to preach and quiz from the Baltimore Catechism. Simple questions, straight-forward answers. "Why did God make you? God made me to know Him, to love Him, and to serve Him in this world, and to be happy with Him forever in heaven." Youngsters were grilled to test whether they were absorbing the basics of their faith.

Girls from St. Mary's went on to attend the Academy of Notre Dame, an all-girl Catholic high school on the west end of town. Boys graduated to Cathedral High School, an all-boy Catholic institution in the center of town. Different settings to be sure, but one thing parents at the time never doubted: girls and boys would get the same Catholic teaching. In these formative years, the focus was on living a good, moral Catholic life which would, of course, always tie back to the fundamentals engrained earlier in grade school. The youths heard clear messages … right was right, wrong was wrong, mortal sin was mortal sin. Heaven was real. And so was Hell.

In these years, Mary formed an impression about her faith that would prove vitally important in later life. As she saw it, the Catholic faith, when studied and tested, simply always made sense. It "added up". Difficult concepts could always be explained by, and aligned with, the Church's teachings. Unbeknownst to her at the time, she was following the tracks of the revered St. John Henry Newman who reached a similar conclusion back in 1840, in route to converting from Anglican to Catholic. Mary didn't have the formal training of Newman, but she had enough sound Catholic education and common sense to recognize the evidence. She also began to trust that sound guidance regarding life's challenges could be found in her faith and in the Church's teachings.

For high school girls daily Mass was not a requirement. Notre Dame's chapel was too small for the student body, so girls were encouraged to attend at their home parish before school. Boys at Cathedral High, on the other hand, still went to Mass together. But for both boys and girls, one bit of their grade school routine did carry over to high school: religion class led by a priest. Priests were tapped from local parishes to accomplish this task. While this might seem a burden on the parish clergy, it really was not. Flush with vocations, parishes routinely had multiple assisting priests in addition to their pastor. St. Mary's was home to two assistant pastors, while five assistants helped support the larger Cathedral parish. And just as Mass was a daily routine, monthly Confession was routine for students (as well as their parents). One might say that being anything short of a rock-solid Catholic youth simply wasn't an option.

SUNDAY MASS AT THE CENTER

Parish life remained an anchor for St. Mary's families throughout the school years, including Thursday night "novena" devotion to Our Lady of Perpetual Help, Sunday afternoon vespers, scouting, and sports teams. But it all centered on Sunday morning when men, women, boys and girls donned their best suits and dresses. The occasion was Holy Mass, where the traditional

Latin Rite Mass would be said exactly as it had been in every Catholic Church around the world for over four hundred years. It was the pinnacle of the worship week, especially for those who attended the High Mass. Parish families filed into church quietly, most adults and children carrying their own personal missals (Latin on the left page, corresponding English on the right). The missals were ready, places marked by colorful ribbons and holy cards to help navigate the day's Mass. The organist began and was joined by the choir. From the sacristy on the left, the priest entered, followed by a team of servers, all young men. For the entire Mass, most verbal exchanges were between the priest, the servers, and the choir. Only the gospel and homily would be spoken in English. Communion was taken kneeling at the long rail in front of the altar. Two long lines down the church's center aisle fed communicants continuously forward to kneel at the rail, where they received the host on their tongues from the priest working his way right to left and then back again along the rail. Everyone lived his own unique experience at the Mass. Some just prayed, paying little attention to the movements on the altar. Others scrambled to keep up with the Latin proceedings while silently reading the prayers in English.

In any case, three things about the High Mass couldn't escape even the most distracted church-goer of the times. First, everything about the church, altar, and movement of persons drew the eye always to Christ on the Cross and to the tabernacle just beneath. The priest's actions contributed to that effect, as he faced the tabernacle almost always during the Mass, and genuflected many times. Second, an object that appeared to be a simple circle of flattened bread was given supreme, other-worldly reverence. And third, regardless of what a person in the pew may be doing or thinking throughout the Mass, he was awash in the majestic singing and Gregorian chant of the choir. Every church-goer, from illiterate tradesman to graduate theologian, took those enriching experiences home on Sunday merely by having been in the church.

Another takeaway from Sunday Mass was a direct and unvarnished message in the pastor's sermon. Father Orlet sternly addressed the days' burgeoning issues for his flock at St. Mary's. The newest scandal of the time was divorce. Among Catholics in Belleville in the 1950's, divorce was virtually unheard of. It is hard to comprehend today just how rare and scandalous was a divorce at that time. Enter the 1960's, and the Belleville News Democrat was cataloguing as many as four or five in the community every week. Once in a while, one of those was a Catholic couple. The very presence of divorce - let alone their increasing number and the unthinkable scandal that any of these were among Catholics - prompted firm words about social morals and Catholic teaching from the pulpit.

GIRL MEETS BOY

On a summer afternoon before her senior year at Notre Dame, Mary and her good friend Jeanine stood at the bus stop after seeing a matinee movie. As fate would have it, a passing car was driven by Jeanine's current crush Milton. In the passenger seat sat his buddy Russ. Both young men were already two years out of Cathedral High School and recently returned home from a tour in the Navy as the war ended. Being gentlemen, they offered the young ladies a ride home, to which the ladies happily assented. Along the way, the four opted to stop at the home of Milton's aunt and uncle where Aunt Marie served sandwiches and supervised a friendly game of six-handed pinochle. Cliché as it seems, the rest is in fact history, and two years later Father Orlet married Russ and Mary at St. Mary's Church.[5]

The newlyweds made home in an apartment over Home Brite, a hardware store just blocks from downtown on Illinois Street. Mary had worked part-time at Home Brite during high school, and the owners were delighted to have the young tenants. For his part, Russ had briefly worked on a farm just outside of town following his service in the Navy, until landing entry-level mechanic work at a chemical company in St. Louis (the same company he would retire from some thirty-five years later). From their new apartment, Russ was commuting to St. Louis as part of a carpool. Mary continued her

---

5 Yes, Jeanine and Milton also married and the four remained lifelong close friends.

work as a bookkeeper downstairs at the hardware store as the two tried to save money for a home. A year later their firstborn arrived. Mary's mother helped by babysitting, an arrangement that worked well except on days Russ needed the car for his turn as driver in the carpool. On those special days, Mary boarded an early-morning city bus with her newborn to ride the 45-minute circuit, dropping off her baby at grandma's house, then completing the circle back to Home Brite to start work. Two years after daughter number one was born, the second arrived. Mary needed to stop working. The apartment was small, as was their bank account. Mary and Russ managed to buy a small two-bedroom home in St. Mary's parish and settled in. Four more children followed. Mary and Russ (and most people those days) plunged into raising a large family while struggling to make ends meet. They were inexperienced, forced to rely on common sense and whatever values and priority systems they had developed in their young lives.[6]

Each of Mary and Russ' children walked through the front doors at St. Mary's Grade School when they turned five years of age. The three oldest children, born in 1950, 1952, and 1953, would experience Catholic grade school much as Mary had 20 years earlier. As for the younger three, change was brewing at Church and school. When 1960 rolled around, their four daughters were ages ten, eight, six, and two. Boy number one had just arrived.

IN A TOWN WHERE THE SQUARE IS A CIRCLE

By 1960, thirty-seven thousand people resided in a growing Belleville, Illinois. Small-town USA, one might say. A drive through town usually included passing through the town square. At The Square, a circular road (actually a roundabout familiar to Europeans, but far less common in the Central U.S.) guided traffic around the town's spectacular central fountain.

---

6 Stretching every penny was a way of life. The young couple decided to spend a generous Christmas bonus from Home Brite (Mary's last before stopping work) on a sewing machine. That machine, and Mary, did a lot of work in the years to come.

Children took special joy in watching Dad steer the car into the two-lane traffic wheel, then find his way out in another direction. Four roads meet at the circle, Illinois Street headed North or South, and Main Street headed East or West.

Main Street west leads to almost two hundred blocks lined with businesses, homes, and neighborhood taverns before meeting Highway 157, where Main Street changes to State Street. That intersection is an almost undetectable cross-over from Belleville into East St. Louis, "Pittsburgh of the West" as it was known at the time ... a neighboring community of 80,000 so respected it was named an All-American City in 1959. Keep driving west on State Street, through downtown East St. Louis, cross a long bridge over the Mississippi, pass by the site of the future Gateway Arch, and St. Louis, Missouri, opens its arms with all its major-city attractions.

Back at Belleville's downtown circle, any direction other than west would yield a far different experience. Drive north, south, or east and the city soon disappears into the rear view mirror. The road tightens to two lanes. Only small towns, farms and railroads mark the land out into southern Illinois.

A real understanding of Belleville - as the 1960's approached - starts with religion. There was no stronger thread in the community's DNA than the Catholic Church. Solid Catholic families, mostly of German ancestry. Mass every Sunday, fish every Friday, and almost never a divorce. Beginning back in 1843, St. Peter's Cathedral served the needs of all Catholics when the town was forming. In 1883 St. Peter's spawned St. Luke's Parish to manage growth in the downtown area. St. Mary's soon followed in 1893, situated prominently on Main Street seventeen blocks west of the Square. Three more parishes and a seminary for young men followed in the 1920's. In the 1950's, with city population nearing 35,000, two more parishes (Mary Queen of Peace and St. Augustine) were added, and more parishes were opened and planned in the fields north of Belleville as neighboring cities formed. Parishes new and old thrived and were readily provided priests. The seminaries were busy, producing bumper crops. Each parish housed a school, staffed mostly by teaching nuns. The nuns played an invaluable role in the parish as without them, private Catholic education would not have been affordable for the large families so common among the congregations.

Flourishing church life had a positive, profound effect on Belleville's overall civic success. Everyone knew the basic morals and priorities of the Catholics, whether subscribing to them or not. This silent force impressed upon daily activity throughout the city. Because of all this, no one would have predicted in 1960 a rapid decline in Belleville's thriving Catholic community. Even more unthinkable was that Belleville could become ground zero for Catholic Church scandal just decades later.

LONG SHADOW OF THE UNIVERSAL CHURCH

Catholic life in 1950's Belleville was like that in most U.S. cities, save for the city's status as a diocesan seat. As such, Belleville was home to a bishop and his cathedral, looming reminders of the Diocese's place within the universal Roman Catholic Church. From the start of his assignment in 1947, Bishop Zuroweste had guided the Diocese of Belleville in much the same way as his fellow bishops around the world. In fact, this was much the same as bishops had done for centuries. The Catholic Church was famously deliberate, which explains how - despite its worldwide reach – the Church had managed to maintain uniformity among dioceses and remarkable continuity over time.

The faithful around the globe took great pride and comfort in knowing that parish life and practices everywhere else were quite similar. Then came the 1960's.

In 1959 Pope John XXIII called for a global ecumenical council of the Church's bishops. It is well-known now as the Second Vatican Council (1962- 1965). Despite knowing little about the Council or why it had been called, Catholics generally welcomed it. They knew councils had been held throughout the history of the Church, and had usually produced positive results. In particular, the many fruits of the Council of Trent (1545-1563) were familiar to, and treasured by, current day Catholics.

And so, relatively few Catholics paid any attention to Vatican II as it opened, paused, and re-convened over the course of those 3 years. They were content with general updates from the Bishop while the Council was underway.

Once the Council closed, implementation of its resolutions was directed from Rome. Bishops (like Zuroweste) received their marching orders, and parish priests (like Father Orlet, now a Monsignor) would in turn receive theirs. The lay faithful were to be herded into a new church, a church strangely anxious to cast aside its slow-moving character of the past.

CHAPTER 2:
CHANGE ROLLS DOWN
MAIN STREET

EVERYONE IN POSITION

With ink still drying on Vatican II documents, Rome began the implementation phase. Church leaders knew significant "innovations" would soon
flow from the Council, and worldwide communications were preemptively
launched to diffuse the arguments of any who might resist. Diocesan publications dutifully published articles like one penned by Father Annibale
Bugnini, appearing in Belleville's diocesan newspaper, The Messenger, in
February of 1965. Father Bugnini was a longtime member of the Roman
Curia and serving as Secretary of the Council for the Implementation of
the Constitution on the Liturgy. In the article Father Bugnini assured the
faithful regarding certain elements of the Holy Mass, saying for example,
"Gregorian chant and sacred music must stay ... rubrics and formulas for
the Eucharistic Prayer remain intact from old ... substantially, nothing will
change in the Missal..." Father Bugnini wasn't well-known at that time. He
would gain fame years later when he emerged as the chief author of the
"New Order of the Mass."[7]

Notwithstanding assurances from Rome, implementation of Vatican
II began sending waves of continuous change rolling down Main Streets

---

7   Spoiler alert: each of those 1965 promises by Father Bugnini about the liturgy would be
broken within five years.

and into parishes around the globe. Bishops were eager to have changes implemented throughout their dioceses. Bishop Zuroweste, like his peers, knew his parish priests well and he knew they would differ greatly in their receptivity. He allowed flexibility in the timing of changes at each parish, but made it clear that they would ultimately happen everywhere.

At St. Mary's the exact sequence of changes stemming from Vatican II may be lost to history, but some records do exist. Some key information has been provided by people who recall in striking detail events that rocked their world between 1965 and 1975. It's worth noting that St. Mary's Parish changed slowly compared to most other parishes. Monsignor Orlet saw to that, because he had never been keen on the revolution.[8]

MASS AND PRAYER

Shortly after the Council, two early developments surfaced at the dinner tables of St. Mary families. The older school children, recapping their day, passed along news that the "Amen" would no longer be said at the end of the Our Father. Soon after that, families received word that all references to the Holy Ghost would now be revised to Holy Spirit. No real explanation for these changes had been given to the children at school. No logical explanation was provided to the few parents who pursued the question further.[9]

It wasn't long before Monsignor Orlet personally announced another change, this time to the gathered congregation at Sunday Mass. According to leaders in Rome, the faithful needed more exposure to the Bible, especially Old Testament teachings. Parishioners really didn't have a big problem with this. Little was said, and a third reading was inserted into the Mass a week later.

---

8 He may have hoped that changes would be reversed and so he could avoid unnecessary upheaval. Or maybe he thought he could somehow shelter his flock from certain elements of the new Church. St. Mary's was eventually forced to comply.

9 In hindsight, some observers believe that small changes like this were introduced merely to begin conditioning the faithful to change itself ... laying the groundwork for more significant innovations to follow.

PARISH LIFE

Life on the parish grounds took on new character. One couldn't help but notice the speedy metamorphosis of the School Sisters of Notre Dame. For over half a century the sisters had devoted themselves humbly to teaching the children at St. Mary's. They resided across the courtyard from the school in a stout three-story red brick convent that joined to the Church on the east side by covered wooden-arched walkways. Life for the SSND nuns until now had revolved around teaching and praying. They seldom left the parish grounds, and were always in the traditional full habit of SSND (ensuring that only their faces could be seen).

Vatican II triggered a sea change among the nuns. They were now going to the front lines of the Church's interaction with society-at-large. For this they would need a new, modern look. Full habits gave way quickly to mid-length skirts, blouses, and half-veils.

Of course, time would have to be made for the nuns' new calling. The time was borrowed from teaching and prayer. And the nuns charged forth into the community.

Across the courtyard, an explosion of adult activity took place from the second-floor gymnasium to the basement cafeterias. On a given night one might find the new parish council meeting in the hot-lunch cafeteria, the new adult volleyball league at play in the gym, and the new liturgy committee meeting in a first-floor classroom. Hardly a function existed within the parish for which a new lay committee hadn't been formed to pursue its grand pinnacle. Hospitality now had a guiding committee, so also music and education, the list goes on.

For the grade school kids (Mary's youngest three were still at St. Mary's), religious education was targeted for major change. Foremost among the goals of those teaching religion was to move away from the Baltimore Catechism, now considered a vestige of Catholic rigidity of the past. At St. Mary's this wasn't an easy task. The Baltimore Catechism was treasured by some long-time parishioners with very stiff spines. Teachers moved to introduce other books and resources. The parents raised their voices in whatever venues they were provided, and succeeded in turning back this one significant change - at least for the time being.

Mary and Russ's three oldest girls were at the Academy of Notre Dame High School when news rocked the city. A priest, a religion teacher at Notre Dame, suddenly announced he was leaving the priesthood. Maybe news of this type would later become routine, but not so in in the late 1960's. Such a thing was unheard of in Mary's lifetime or in her parents' lifetime. Priesthood, for ages the unshakeable core of the Catholic Church, was cracking at its foundation.

Mary took note of all this. And her concern grew.

TENSION IN THE PEWS

Most Sunday mornings in the mid-1960's, Mary and her family climbed the stairs to the church balcony, walked over to the aisle, and then forward and down into the second pew. Russ slid the brim of his hat under a bronze clip on back of the first pew. The location was familiar and comfortable; the air among the congregation was anything but. Ongoing, significant changes on the altar and in the school were being absorbed quite differently by the people of the parish.

Some parishioners, a sizable contingent, were enthusiastic about changes. Others were amenable to changes, either believing their Bishop's direction needn't be questioned or not engaged enough to have an informed opinion. Mary and Russ were in a third camp - likely the smallest. They were willing to go along for the time being, though apprehensive about what lay ahead. In any case, those in St. Mary's pews at this time were obedient … they would follow directives and hope the virtue of changes could be understood over time.

CONFUSION RUNS RAMPANT - HUMANAE VITAE

As ongoing waves of Vatican II changes washed into parishes everywhere, Rome added to the confusion. For decades progressives in the Church had sought an end to the Church's staunch opposition to artificial contraception. Introduction of the birth control pill in 1960 had recently thrown gas on that fire. Not wanting his upcoming Vatican II Council to be consumed by this issue, Pope John XXIII established the Pontifical Commission on Birth Control in 1963 to study the subject separately. Three years later, and now in the pontificate of Paul VI, the commission produced its report, recommending to the Pope that artificial contraception be approved by the Church. It was a Commission report with recommendations, but nothing was final: any official, authoritative action was strictly the prerogative of the Pope.

Pope Paul VI did take action in 1968, stunning the Catholic world with his encyclical Humanae Vitae. It had been widely expected that he would accept the Pontifical Commission's recommendations. He did exactly the opposite. Humanae Vitae reaffirmed the Catholic Church's long-standing view of marriage and marital relations and condemned artificial contraception. Conservative, traditional Catholics rejoiced at the news. Progressives were in disbelief.

The message of Humanae Vitae was in perfect continuity with traditional teaching. It was clear, without ambiguity. The encyclical should have served as a calming effect in the nervous times of the late 1960's and it would have ... if it had been dutifully accepted by Church leaders (notably bishops, theologians, and priests). Unfortunately, leading reformers in the Church, emboldened by their success at Vatican II, denounced the encyclical. They refused to recognize it as authoritative, opting to ignore it and pressing ahead with their pro-contraception beliefs in the seminaries and in the public arena. Church leadership was radically split in an area of morality that has always been central to man's flourishing - human sexuality.

It wasn't long before this conflict reverberated down through the parishes. Messages from the pulpit and from behind the confessional screen about reproductive issues were now unpredictable. Truth – the Church's treasure, and the one thing Catholics needed – no longer came in black and white. All was relative. Mary saw this. Her fellow parishioners saw this. Confusion flourished. Mary's concern mounted.

LITURGY MOVES IN

Entering the late 1960's Monsignor Orlet was under pressure from the Bishop to implement more changes. He resolved to announce yet another change to his flock at Sunday Mass. Following his homily, with the sunlight flooding through St. Mary's renowned stained glass windows, Monsignor Orlet told the congregation that the priest would be turning around to face them during the Mass. In order to make this possible, a new table would be installed in front of the high altar. Murmur filled the church. Monsignor Orlet explained, as he would on several future occasions of change, that this was experimental and that the Church would likely reverse this approach after its trial. The faithful, harboring a wide range of emotions about another new practice within the Mass, gulped and followed orders.[10]

Then from the pulpit in the summer of 1969, Monsignor Orlet delivered news he had hoped would never come. The New Order Mass, crafted by committees formed out of the Second Vatican Council, had been finalized and was mandatory. The "Novus Ordo" Mass was to replace the Traditional Latin Mass on the first day of Advent in the fall of 1969. Monsignor stated that St. Mary's would comply, it was their duty. He knew he was bidding farewell to the traditional Mass he had so often described to his flock as "perfect." This caused in him a heavy grief.

November 30, 1969 was brisk but sunny as parishioners filed into St. Mary's Church for the first official celebration of the New Order Mass.

---

10   Little did they know the Catholic Church's brief, recent history of priests facing the congregation. In Holland in 1965, some priests had begun this practice in imitation of Protestant services. When the Vatican discovered this, they quickly issued notice that the practice was NOT approved. The Vatican's direction was ignored. The practice spread quickly through Europe and internationally thereafter, despite the fact that no Vatican II document to date had authorized this.

Catholics had a very new Mass. More precisely, they had a new *Liturgy,*[11] as it was now to be called.

The Sacrifice of the Holy Mass has been the pinnacle of Catholic worship for two thousand years. Prior to 1969, the Traditional "Tridentine" Latin Rite had been in use, literally without change for over 400 years - since the Council of Trent managed to standardize into one Rite various existing forms in use in the 1500's. It should not be surprising that change to the longstanding Mass, especially extensive change formulated and implemented in a short period of time as was happening with Vatican II, would be controversial. Mountains of literature exist on this subject, but for the purposes of this story, several facts are critical:

- Incremental changes made up until fall of 1969, some introduced as experimental, were now permanently ensconced. One clear example of this was the priest facing the congregation from behind a "table," which was now standard practice.[12] The hopes of some laypersons, that experimental practices would be reversed, had been dashed. And to some it confirmed suspicion that an intentional, incremental, even deceptive rollout had been happening since the mid-1960's.

- The Holy Mass would be said in English at St. Mary's (and in countless other vernacular languages worldwide). To most in the congregation it seemed an interesting idea. To some it was even exciting. Still others thought it an unnecessary and/or unwelcome change. One thing was for sure, the Catholic Church would seem a little less "universal" without its Latin.

- Rubrics and formulas for the Eucharistic Prayer were re-written. It was clear to observers that this contradicted Father Bugnini's 1965 assurances ("Gregorian chant and sacred music must stay ... rubrics

---

11 The term "liturgy" was to replace "Mass." To some observers at the time this bore an eerie likeness to Protestantism.

12 The New Rite does not formally require that the priest face the faithful during the Mass. In fact, it includes several instructions to the priest to "turn and face the faithful". Obviously, this instruction only makes sense if the priest is, at that moment, facing away from them.

and formulas for the Eucharistic Prayer remain intact from old ... substantially, nothing will change in the Missal...""). Every one of these was now proven false.[13]

- Missals from the 1962 Rite of the Mass were no longer applicable. New, disposable monthly missalettes and new hymnals were issued.

- A Sign of Peace was inserted immediately before Holy Communion. It was welcomed by many as a nice social gesture to others near them at Mass.

In a nutshell, Mary saw the Novus Ordo Mass[14] as stripping away the sacredness of the Mass she'd been raised with. Further, it seemed much of this had been implemented deceptively. Her confusion and concern were skyrocketing.

MODERN MUSIC TAKES THE STAGE

Music plays a unique and important role in the Solemn Traditional Latin Mass, where sacred music is sung by a choir frequently accompanied by pipe organ. The sacred music was actually singing of the prayers of the Mass in traditional Gregorian chant, a practice that had endured for many centuries. In the low Mass, there had been no music at all, though this had changed slightly in the 1950's, when the faithful began to sing traditional hymns at certain points as the priest prayed silently.

Of course, music is also important in the New Order Mass, though its nature has become quite different from the Latin Mass. During the implementation of Vatican II, music transitioned virtually overnight from singing

---

13 Reference: 1969 Apostolic Constitution ... "The major innovation concerns the Eucharistic Prayer."

14 Other notable background regarding development of the New Order of the Mass: Among Father Bugnini's advisors when developing the New Mass were five Protestants. Catholics were unaware that the "proposed" New Rite had originally been celebrated before a gathering of Bishops in the Sistene Chapel, for their appraisal and comment, on October 24, 1967. The next day, only 71 of the 176 bishops who attended voted "yes" for the New Rite, the rest voting "no" or having reservations. Votes were never solicited from other bishops. Undeterred by this rejection, the champions of the New Rite pushed forward to its 1969 rollout without substantive change.

the Mass (prayers) to singing at Mass (hymns).[15] Modern hymns dominated the new Mass. So fast was their adoption that almost every Sunday the faithful were subjected to singing lessons led by the music director before Mass to rehearse the week's new tune(s). Magnificent pipe organs were mothballed, pushed aside by piano and other instruments. Gregorian chant vanished from Catholic Churches during the season of Advent, 1969.[16]

All these changes in music were adopted at St. Mary's. As with other changes, some of the faithful were happy. But the move to modern music was a huge blow to people like Mary. To her, it was an assault on the aspirational, heavenly atmosphere her church once offered.

CHURCH FACELIFT

Up until the 1960's, St. Mary's parishioners enjoyed one of the finest traditional Catholic Church settings in southern Illinois.

Then in the 1960's the church interior began to transform in order to accommodate changes being made in the liturgy. Most notably, the high altar at the tabernacle was replaced by a stone table, separate from and in front of the tabernacle, enabling the priest to face the faithful during Mass, as shown in this 1970 photo:

---

15 The Novus Ordo Mass was rolled out without Gregorian chants having been written for its new rites.

16 It is worth noting that changes in music at the Mass, specifically the sudden disappearance of Gregorian chant, weren't by any order of the New Mass. Sacrosanctum Concillium, the very first constitution promulgated by Vatican II in 1963 specifically stated that Gregorian chant is "specially suited to the Roman liturgy" and that "Gregorian chant should have first place among all legitimate types of sacred music."

St. Mary's Church – 1970

But by 1973, a new pastor was in place at St. Mary's. Early in his tenure, he sketched up designs for a church interior to fully complement the innovative New Mass of which he was a fervent advocate. Though few parishioners were even aware of plans when the project was announced, notice was served that Mass would be held in the school Gymnasium for three months while renovations were made to the church. These renovations produced a Sanctuary with a very new look:

St. Mary's Church - 1993

Most obvious are the absence of the communion rail, the missing high altar at the rear center of the sanctuary, the "risen Jesus" in lieu of the Crucifix high on the center wall, a smaller and simpler table in the center, no canopy of any sort above the priest, the blank walls that previously held Blessed Virgin Mary and St. Joseph statues in customary side-altar locations left and right of the sanctuary, and most chilling of all - the Tabernacle itself gone from sight. It was impossible for Mary to understand why changes like this were necessary. For her, ageless and beautiful features that once defined a truly majestic place for our Lord's Mass had been needlessly ripped away. A barren, Protestantized stage had taken its place.

CHAPTER 3:

POINT OF RECKONING

REACHING OUT

Recall that from the earliest signs of change at St. Mary's, Mary and Russ were among those willing to go along but apprehensive about what lay ahead. But by the late 1960's, many actions taken by the Church didn't make sense to them. The Church seemed to be leaving behind things the Church itself had earlier taught them to hold sacred. Mary kept reflecting on the impression she'd held since her youth … Catholicism ALWAYS made sense; it always added up. She was anxious and confused now, but believed there HAD to be good reasons for all these changes. She was determined to understand them. Unfortunately, looking around for support, she saw few fellow parishioners displaying the same level of concern. Even Russ was less inclined to worry about it. Still in her thirties and rearing a young family, Mary grasped for answers.

In 1969, everyone's attention was on the New Order Mass. But almost all Catholics, rather than questioning any changes, were devoted to implementing the New Mass and achieving universal acceptance of it. To that end, in Belleville at least, evening meetings were held to introduce and discuss the New Mass and its reasoning. When notice of meetings at St. Mary's appeared in the weekly bulletins, Mary jumped at the chance. One session was run by a diocesan priest who possessed an impressive priestly resume; ordained in Rome, schooled at the Pontifical Gregorian University in Rome (for Theology) and then at St. Louis University (for Scripture), by 1969 a Scripture Scholar for the Diocese of Belleville. An exchange with this priest at an evening meeting left a lifelong impression on Mary. She had recently been to a Lutheran funeral service, where she'd been struck by the similarity between that Lutheran service and the approach now being followed in the New Order Mass at St. Mary's. She made that point, to which he replied, "What is wrong with Luther?" It wasn't intended as a joke. Mary froze in her tracks. She'd been taught her whole life there was much wrong with Luther and the Protestant Reformation he led. She returned home that night with the impression the Catholic clergy was turning Protestant.

Yet another parish meeting produced another memorable exchange, this one with a fellow parishioner. Mary was fairly sure she was the lone skeptic of the New Mass in a tiny classroom this one evening. Even so, she rounded up the courage to ask at one point "Why can't we just have the Old Mass?" A man she had known for 20 years (with whom she'd always been on friendly terms) snapped a sharp reply, "Why would we want to go back to that old stuff?" The entire classroom bellowed support, and there was to be no more discussion of the topic. It was clear … the advocates of change were on a mission and would not stand for challenges. Mary was alone, or so it seemed, and people like her were quickly being branded "rabble-rousers." These forums were no place to look for answers or help.

Meanwhile Mary also sought answers in the confessional. Considering the many priests assisting at St. Mary's, she really didn't know what to expect them to offer as guidance. In her first attempt, Mary asked the priest behind the curtain whether the Traditional Latin Mass could be said as an alternative to the Novus Ordo Mass. He didn't provide a direct answer, but he did suggest she take two actions. First, she should read a book which he would lend to her.[17] Second, he suggested she read the actual documents from Vatican II. Well, maybe some people would consider reading Vatican documents too daunting a task, but not Mary. She plunged into them, starting with the

---

17 He did later provide the book, which proved to be no more than a presentation of the wonders of the Novus Order Mass.

document on the Liturgy.[18] Just four paragraphs into the Introduction, she came across words that would echo in her mind for decades to come:

> " … in faithful obedience to Tradition, the Sacred Council declares that holy Mother Church holds all lawfully acknowledged rites to be of equal right and dignity; that she wishes to preserve them in the future and to foster them in every way."

Mary was a great student, and she reviewed the liturgy documents carefully. She found that nothing in them suggested that the Traditional Latin Mass was to be left behind. In fact, Vatican II documents *encouraged* the continuation of traditional rites.

She now felt the clergy were not being honest about what Vatican II had produced and what was now happening in the parish churches. This discovery shocked her and steeled her resolve.

Not one to resign easily, Mary later questioned another priest in the confessional about prospects for the Latin Mass being said again at St. Mary's. This time the answer was quite direct. She was told, "If you go to a Latin Mass it will be a mortal sin." The message from the local clergy seemed bold and unsympathetic, in effect, "Get over the Latin Mass, and get on board with the new Church." But it didn't make sense.

Try as she may, Mary could not get an answer from anyone in the clergy to the simple question, "Why can't we have the Latin Mass?" Mystery surrounded the case. Eventually, Mary became haunted by that confessional message and she had to know , "How would it be a mortal sin to attend the Latin Mass one day (after the Novus Ordo had been introduced), when before the Novus Ordo was introduced, it would have been a mortal sin NOT to go to the Latin Mass?" "Surely," she thought, "the Latin Mass itself couldn't have been that wrong, for so long." It didn't make sense; it didn't add up. And as we know, to her mind the Catholic Church had always made sense. Mary

---

18 Sacrosanctum Concillium was the first document issued by the Second Vatican Council, promulgated by Pope Paul VI on December 4, 1963. The document was approved by a vote of 2,147 to 4.

poured over her copy of The Messenger every week, searching for some kind of official document that explained the disappearance of the Latin Mass.

Mary contemplated taking the issue to Monsignor Orlet. She had always been a humble Catholic, not inclined to take issues such as this directly to a pastor, face-to-face. Now was different, she was emboldened. But one fact did intervene. Monsignor Orlet was in failing health, and she decided she would not trouble her long-trusted pastor. She also considered approaching Bishop Zuroweste. For her, this was a daunting prospect. It was one thing to be a "rabble-rouser" at the parish, but for a Catholic raised in Mary's generation, taking her Bishop to task would still be a bridge too far. For the time being she saw no course other than to continue going to Mass and praying for answers.

Mary was increasingly upset, but still resigned to the idea that Church direction must be obeyed. She did find other opportunities to reach out for answers or explanation. At Russ' suggestion, she registered for a 3-day retreat held at King's House in the Fall of 1971. King's House is the diocesan retreat center located on 48 wooded acres at the west end of Belleville. All King's House retreats in those days were held in its two-story main building, where the first floor contained offices, a cafeteria, and a chapel doubling also as the primary meeting place. Modest guest rooms for retreatants are in an adjacent three-story residential wing, and across the street is a smaller stone building for offices and a library.

Mary brought one overriding question with her to King's House: "Is all this change in the Church OK?" She hoped the retreat director might crack the code for her.

The retreat kicked off Friday afternoon with Mass in the first floor chapel. Several hours of conferences then followed in the evening. The priest bore an uncanny resemblance to Jack Benny, and he acted a lot like the well-known comedian. While his mannerisms and jokes didn't seem very fitting for a retreat director, Mary settled in to see what substance emerged. Her wait was a short one. The priest posed and then discussed theories that were mostly foreign to what Mary had learned over the years. One of his observations really set her back in her seat: "It is nearly impossible to commit a mortal sin. You would have to stand on top of a tall mountain and shout to the sky 'God I reject you completely.'" A restless night of sleep followed for Mary. Saturday morning picked up where Friday evening had left off. Mass led to conferences, and by the time a late-morning break arrived, Mary was in need of a diversion. Recalling the King's House library, shown to them as a resource, she wondered if that diocesan book trove held any literature that could enlighten her. She veered out of the room, down the tile hallway, past the cafeteria, out the side door, across the gravel drive, and into the stone building. The library was just inside the door on the left and she pressed open the door. Having spent a great deal of time in libraries, Mary considered this one to be mid-sized. Books on two walls, a center table and a couple chairs paired with side tables and reading lights. Mary was focused on finding a book about the Mass, something that would explain why it had changed so dramatically in recent years. She loved books and couldn't help but roam around and thumb through a number of them. In time, she found a variety of books about the Mass and took a seat to review them more closely. Several books into the project, something dawned on her. She had not found anywhere in this library a book about the Mass published before Vatican II. No "old" books at all. A cold shudder overtook her and she froze in place. The library had been purged of any books that referenced (or reverenced) the Traditional Latin Mass, though it had been the only Catholic Mass just a few years earlier. Mary returned the books to their places on the shelves and walked slowly back to the conference which was back in session. She was committed to stay at the retreat until its end on Sunday, but her findings in the library, Jack Benny's leadership, and the general teachings at the retreat all combined to magnify her growing angst.

CHANGE ROLLS ON

Through the mid-1970's waves of change continued to roll down Main Street, right through the front doors of St. Mary's. Almost everything was affected.

- **Revisions to the Catholic funeral Mass**[19]**and practices at funeral wakes.** Mary encountered these on an ongoing basis. On one occasion, Mary attended a wake for a St. Augustine parishioner (neighboring parish to St. Mary's) where the newspaper had placed notice the rosary would be said for the deceased. They didn't say the rosary at this wake, and afterward Mary asked the pastor why they hadn't. His response could only be interpreted as his belief that no one wanted to say the rosary at funerals any more.On another occasion, Mary saw an RCIA[20] class advertised in St. Mary's bulletin inviting anyone interested in the Catholic Church or wanting to know about it. It would be held in the basement at St. Mary's and, ever inquisitive, Mary attended. At some point the subject of the rosary surfaced and Mary asked why the rosary was no longer said at Catholic wakes. This priest's reply was, "It sounds like geese clacking." In addition to scuttling the rosary, Catholic wakes trended to more scripture readings and commentary, something that struck Mary as mimicking Protestant practice.

- **Revised rules regarding penance.** Prior to Vatican II the rules for penance, including fasting and abstinence were crystal clear and practiced worldwide. One example relates to Friday penance. It was defined as abstaining from meat on all regular Fridays of the year,

---

19 Here, Father Bugnini's influence is felt again. He explained that the reforms "got rid of texts that smacked of a negative spirituality inherited from the Middle Ages. Thus they removed such familiar and even beloved texts as the *Libera me, Domine*, the *Dies irae*, and others that overemphasized judgment, fear, and despair. These they replaced with texts urging Christian hope and giving more effective expression to faith in the resurrection." Ref: *The Reform of the Liturgy* p. 773

20 The Rite of Christian Initiation of Adults (RCIA), or Ordo Initiationis Christianae Adultorum (OICA) is a process developed by the Catholic Church for prospective converts to Catholicism who are above the age of infant baptism. Candidates are gradually introduced to aspects of Catholic beliefs and practices.

and failure to abide was considered "gravely sinful" by the Church. Then in 1966, following direction from the United States Bishops, this requirement was modified in the U.S. to allow each person to define the Friday penance however they pleased.[21]

- **Receiving of the Holy Eucharist.** The Holy Eucharist was now to be received standing up. At St. Mary's Church, the pastor first introduced the idea as a solution to his predicament of the moment (he had injured himself and was on crutches). When standing communion remained as a permanent practice at St. Mary's, it was clear that the centuries-old act of kneeling was being discarded. Mary gulped again, struggling to comprehend this change to the most sacred personal moment of the Holy Mass.

- **Lay lectors.** Traditionally all Biblical readings had been proclaimed by a priest. Now, lay persons were approved to read the first and second passages, leaving only the Gospel for the ordained. In the name of more participation (encouraged by Vatican II), these lectors represented a more active role for the laity in the sanctuary.

- **Continuing evolution of music at the liturgy.** All guardrails came off with respect to music at the liturgy. A cottage industry exploded for writing and performing modern hymns. Instruments previously considered unfit for use in a church were now welcome. Youth masses proliferated, featuring all types of music from folk to rock. Musicians were frequently relocated from the balcony to high-visibility positions near the front of Church. A friend of Mary's played guitar in one of those groups at St. Mary's. He enjoyed it for a period of time, but began to wonder if this music was truly suited for Mass. His moment of truth happened after a Mass when a fellow parishioner requested that the musicians "move around more to better entertain." He reflected on that input and decided instead to move

---

21 It need not be abstinence from meat, but some form of penance was still required. Catholics were left to decide for themselves. Skeptics worried that without a clearly stated practice the faithful would eventually slide in their penance.

the performers back to the balcony. Not much later, he personally retreated even further (to the pews), having decided to reserve his musical skills to social events.

Most parishioners continued to accept changes as they came. Some actively supported them. Others simply went along. Mary, on the other hand, took exception to almost all of these developments. She just couldn't help feeling more confused, lonely, and upset.

PRIESTS IN THE CROSS-FIRE

Caught in the cross-fire of Vatican II's implementation were priests who did not agree with its revolutionary changes. One of them was the beloved pastor at St. Mary's, Monsignor Joseph Orlet. Ultimately, he had been obedient to his Bishop and guided his flock into the "new" Church. He grieved over this, especially the loss of the Latin Mass. His grief never ended, but he was at least taken from it by death just three years after the Novus Order arrived at St. Mary's.

To be sure, there were other priests who revered Tradition the way Monsignor Orlet had. They too mourned the loss of traditions they believed were essential to a strong Church. They didn't know what lay ahead for them individually, but knew it was likely to be difficult.[22] Standing squarely in the path of any individual priest who desired to express reverence for Tradition were the power-brokers. In the Catholic Church, these are the Bishops. As descendants of the apostles, they direct the Church – for better or worse. At this point, Mary shivered to think whether there was even one Bishop on earth who believed in Tradition and in the Latin Mass.

---

22 Some of them would go on to be "Embers" themselves. And eventually Mary's path would cross with some of theirs.

EMBER AT A CROSSROAD

The ongoing change at St. Mary's was never far from mind, but Mary's first priority during those years was keeping the household running on a tight budget. Six kids to get through school. The oldest was gifted on the piano, next came a band member, then a singer, a cheerleader and two boys in year-round sports. All the girls played piano (thanks to Aunt Freida's donated piano), practicing between lessons given by Sr. Doralice. For years Mary oversaw scales, spotted jumps, coached techniques, shuttled players, made costumes, and caught endless balls in the time she could carve out from groceries, cooking, cleaning, washing, and sewing. Russ' paycheck from the chemical plant covered the growing family's bills with little to spare. His bacon and eggs were ready every morning at 5:45 and his children awaited his, "Howdy-do, howdy-do!" greeting every evening at 4:30 as he walked in the front door. Dinner followed promptly at 5:00. Russ would relax in the evening as much as possible, considering he was always on call. There were many calls, and frequent late-night drives back to St. Louis, some keeping him in St. Louis straight through his day shift. Life at home was hectic but happy. Yet for Mary, concerns about the Catholic Church were lurking, waiting to be addressed. That opportunity surfaced as soon as the kids were all in school.

She started by questioning whether she had simply grown up believing what her parents wanted her to believe. This meant taking time to study the fundamentals of other religions. Of particular interest were the Mormon and Lutheran faiths. Every day for months, in whatever time she could spare while the kids were at school, she would pour over books and documents to understand more about who started these religions and what they believed. In the end, she arrived right back where she started. Every other religion fell short on the most critical measures. The Catholic faith went straight back to Christ who was God, and He had started His Church to carry out the building of His kingdom on earth. The apostolic chain had protected the one true religion. It made sense. It added up.

Having affirmed her commitment to Catholicism, Mary realized she now faced a problem long in the making. The staggering changes since Vatican II were re-shaping the Church into something different than the Church from which she'd learned her Catholic faith. In fact, the Church even seemed to be pulling her *away* from the faith she'd learned and held dearly. She worried if there would come a point where the two would be incompatible. Would she have to choose? Would she even have a choice? Sundays were especially difficult for her, struggling through ever-changing Novus Ordo Masses with her family. She'd often walk out in tears. As she always had, Mary looked to her faith to steer her. "If you pray, and pray hard enough, you get answers," she was always taught. So she prayed. Hard.

Her answer came in 1977. In order to "validate man's dignity" it was said, the pastor announced that the Holy Eucharist could be received in the hand (rather than on the tongue) and launched an educational campaign to encourage that new practice.[23] This act was unthinkable to Mary. It brought into question whether the Church truly believed in the living presence of God in the Holy Eucharist.[24] So much of the Mass' ritual was devoted to ensuring that ordained hands, with carefully cleaned fingertips, were the only object to touch the host! And so serious had the obligation of the priest and server been to avoiding the loss of even one fragment of a host! She wondered whether a priest who would distribute communion in the hand could even himself believe in the real presence.[25] Over and above all previous "innovations" since the Second Vatican Council, this change was to Mary a sign that the Church was choosing to be man-centered rather than

---

23 Catholics were generally unaware of recent events surrounding Communion in the hand. In 1968, Communion in the hand was introduced in Holland as an ecumenical gesture. This abuse spread to Germany, Belgium, and France. In 1969 Pope Paul VI issued Memoriale Domini (MD) clarifying that Communion on the tongue was the only approved standard. This was summarily ignored by Bishops and Communion in the hand spread around the world.

24 Shortly thereafter the Catholic Church introduced lay Extraordinary Eucharistic Ministers, further convincing the proponents of Tradition that the modern Church wished to de-emphasize the real presence of Christ in the Eucharist.

25 Ref: The True Story of Communion in the Hand Revealed Luisella Scrosati / One Peter Five / May 8, 2018

God-centered. She had long dreaded this day might come, and now it had. The Catholic Church was clearly unmoored from the faith she held. And as she saw it, the Novus Ordo Mass could not constitute the Holy Mass of the One, True, Catholic, and Apostolic Church.

Mary continued praying. At age 46, she began saying the rosary daily.

PART TWO:
PERSONAL SURVIVAL

A lone Ember, burning passionately with traditional Catholicism. Could someone like this find a place to nurture her faith?

CHAPTER 4:
PRELUDE TO PEACE

Mary was an Ember, and in the Catholic world of 1977 there was no clear path for an Ember to follow. She was left to rely on her beliefs, experiences, and personal acquaintances – most of which have been mentioned. But there are a few events and people that still need to be introduced, key developments in the years just before 1977.

A TRAIL APPEARS

The long-fought battle in St. Mary's classrooms to replace the Baltimore Catechism was finally won by the teachers in 1975. The Baltimore Catechism was being dropped. Mary's youngest child was in the seventh grade. As usual, the school held evening meetings for parishioners to learn about these changes. Mary attended and listened without protesting, sure by now there was nothing to be gained by it. At one of those meetings a practical idea did occur to her, so she waited for the meeting to end and approached the nun who had run the meeting. Mary asked whether she could be given the copies of the Baltimore Catechism that were no longer needed by the school. In yet another display of disdain by those leading change at the parish, the nun replied, "If you want a Baltimore Catechism, go the Catholic Supply House and buy it." This one incident, perhaps more because of its symbolism than its substance, sent Mary home more broken-hearted than other similar incidents had in the past. It also triggered a sequence of events that would, in great part, shape the rest of her life.

At home later, still reeling from the nun's contempt, Mary felt the need to reach out with a message to a woman in the parish who, like her, had long opposed the changes happening at St. Mary's.[26] She phoned that friend and told her flatly, "You were right about what they were trying to do with the catechism." The two exchanged just a few thoughts, including a passing remark by Mary about her willingness to "go anywhere for a Traditional Latin Mass," then said cordial goodbyes.

Mary was busy cleaning house the next day when her phone rang. An unfamiliar female voice greeted her, a woman introducing herself as Judy Hickey. Getting right to the point, Judy explained that she'd heard about Mary's desire to attend a Latin Mass. It was her pleasure, Judy said, to tell her about a Traditional Latin Mass scheduled to be held at the Holiday Inn hotel on Highway 44 at Hampton Avenue in St. Louis at 7:00 p.m. on Thanksgiving night. Surprised and a bit confused, Mary made notes on her phone-side pad but didn't think of the many questions she might normally have asked. Judy hadn't given any indication of where she had heard of Mary, or who was organizing the event. Nor had she offered Mary a ride or even left a phone number. The critical information – time and place - had been delivered, and the call ended as unexpectedly as it had started.

So it was that Mary planned a trip to St. Louis on Thanksgiving night of 1975, to attend her first Traditional Latin Mass (TLM) in six years. Russ was focused on the family's holiday gathering and football games, and she intended to go alone. Mary's mother heard about the planned solo trip and offered to accompany her. The two left after an early Thanksgiving dinner, driving west into the early fall sunset. Thirty-five miles later, in southwest St. Louis, they exited from Highway 44 onto Hampton Avenue. Just two left turns were needed to get them to the Holiday Inn where they maneuvered to the front of the half-empty parking lot. Mary and her mother stepped along the short sidewalk, up to the glass front doors, and entered a spacious and sparsely decorated lobby. On a corner wall opposite the registration desk

26 Resisters were few and, because they tended to hold varying views, they seldom collaborated.

they spotted the first of several hand-written paper signs guiding them to the room reserved for their group.

They were among the first to enter the conference room, walls bare, folding chairs arranged in rows - about ten across and four deep. Centered at the front of the room was a cloth-covered table. On the table sat a three-foot-high cross facing into the room. A candle burned at each side of the table. Mary and her mother sat for half an hour while about 30 people made their way quietly into the room, most carrying their personal Latin-to-English missals. One couldn't help but notice the women and girls in chapel veils, men and boys in ties and jackets. Mass began. It was a low Mass[27], lasting 45 minutes. The priest faced the cross almost the entire Mass, his back to the faithful in their folding chairs. Attendees who were physically able knelt on the floor during the requisite portions of the Mass. Everyone knelt for communion, receiving the Holy Eucharist on the tongue. One precise moment in the Mass has been forever frozen into Mary's mind. As the priest uttered the words consecrating the Holy Eucharist - words spoken in Latin while she followed in her cherished prayer book - she thought to herself, "I'm home; this is where I need to be."

As she and her mother filed out the back of the conference room after Mass, Mary leaned to the man next to her asking whether he knew who had organized the Mass. He welcomed her question and gestured toward a slim young lady in the left rear corner of the room. Mary veered that direction, noting from the activity in the corner that the woman surely knew many of those who had come out this evening. In the center of that action stood Peggy Meuhlemann, greeting her friends as they passed by while keeping an eye on her seven children, ages three to seventeen, now racing around the room. Mary introduced herself and her mother and thanked Peggy for making possible the evening's Mass. Hearing how Mary had received word of the Mass, Peggy was quick to point out Judy Hickey and Mary hurried off to the back door to greet her also. Judy was accompanied by her husband and his mother and grandmother. Trying not to delay their families, the two

---

27   This St. Louis group did not have the infrastructure needed for a High Mass.

agreed to phone again soon and everyone headed into the hall. So high were Mary's spirits they weren't even dampened by her mother's contrary appraisal as they walked out the glass front doors, "I must say, I prefer the New Mass."

JOURNEY OF A FELLOW EMBER

Back in the conference room, Peggy Muehlemann and her kids were finishing chores – candles doused, cross packed, altar coverings removed, and chairs folded. Once the altar was carried out the door and into the van, mom fired up the engine for the thirty minute drive home. Her passengers were tired tonight, so chatter was light. Peggy was left to steer and think. She loved these evenings, especially when she met newcomers like Mary. They usually turned out to be kindred spirits who'd suffered the sudden loss of a treasured church life, spent years searching for answers, and felt the same angst. Even so, their journeys were unique and interesting. Peggy's thoughts drifted back in time to her own odyssey of the past several years. Images of those times came flashing in front of her like a movie in the van's oversized windshield …

The first scene to capture her mind was happy – if a little crazy. It was dinner time in the home she and her husband, Ed, were running in the mid-1960's. At this point there were four little mouths to feed. Money was a little tight for the young and growing family, but they made ends meet. Life around the house was becoming hectic, even more so each time a newborn was added to the clan. Through all of this, somehow there was a sense of order in the home. The older kids behaved respectfully and were taking on new responsibilities. Everyone followed the rules. And in this house the key rules emanated from the central tenets of the Catholic faith; God comes first, love others, tell the truth. Peggy wouldn't have it any other way, and Ed - himself not even Catholic - liked the home environment they were building. For outside support, they needed look no further than their local Catholic church. At St. Martin De Porres, Peggy knew her kids would get timely sacraments and see Catholic fundamentals in action just as generations had before them.

The simplicity and certainty of that first scene gave way as the late 60's approached. Things were shifting at their outside support source, St. Martin De Porres. Out with traditional practices, in with new … one at a time, but steadily. Peggy was confused and upset. By the time her children were starting school, she'd lost confidence that the parish school would develop their Catholic faith in the time-proven way she'd been schooled. The Muehlemann children were sent to public schools. Their faith would be taught and nurtured at home. The family continued attending Sunday Mass at St. Martin De Porres but the experience grew more troubling with time. Then the Novus Ordo Mass arrived in 1969. Recalling the turmoil of that period, a new vision emerges in front of her …

Peggy and her family have entered the vestibule at St. Martin De Porres Church for Sunday Mass. Most of her fellow parishioners are flowing through the vestibule and into church as they always have. A number of them, however, are noticeably animated. They greet others and buzz together about the new innovations being spawned by their various parish committees and the new ministries being launched in the community. Peggy shivers. She hasn't made sense of all the changes happening throughout the parish. She still doesn't see why it's all necessary. She's been patient. Looking for answers that can't be found, she wishes she had options but none are apparent. Mass starts then finishes, a couple new wrinkles having been inserted this week. As the family car nears the parking lot exit, it dawns on Peggy that she is finally in complete agreement with the gentleman often standing at that exit with a small sign, "Welcome to our 'New Mess.'" Peggy can no longer in good conscience attend the New Mass. The Muehlemanns resign from their parish church. She hasn't given up on the Catholic faith, but she has given up on the local Catholic Church as its vehicle. Her mission now is to find the Church she's known all her life… if it's still out there.

Gradually Peggy connected with a few other parishioners who were also concerned about the situation. The common desire among them was for the Traditional Latin Mass. Of course, they yearned for many other traditional practices and disciplines of the church as well, but the all-critical centerpiece was the Latin Mass. If only they could find the Latin Mass once again, other pieces would fall back into place. To that end, the small network of allies would share any information they happened upon. Their clandestine efforts actually did produce some successes. By word of mouth, they discovered a few rare opportunities to attend Latin Mass. These moments typically arose from the efforts of elderly priests who still held a deep love for the "old Mass." Not surprisingly, local priests almost never fit this bill. Occasionally however, a priest from elsewhere - acting as a freelancer - would agree to visit.[28] Mass was offered only at a private location, either at Peggy's home or occasionally at the home of one other couple. These were life-sustaining occasions for the small groups of faithful, but they happened infrequently and sometimes on very short notice. And as one might imagine, the word-of-mouth network occasionally chased opportunities that didn't pan out as expected. Not all paths led to orthodox priests, and humble retreat was sometimes required. These years were frustrating for Peggy, despite the rays of hope that appeared now and then. It was a period of time she was glad to banish from her thoughts as she fast-forwarded her windshield movie to a Sunday in 1973.

The new picture coming into focus for Peggy is a church pew on the quiet campus of the Missionaries of La Salette situated along the Mississippi River well south of the Gateway Arch. The family is a good hour from their home in north county, but the drive this day was anything but a burden. They are able to attend the Traditional Latin Mass every Sunday, something they'd spent four long years hoping for. Once again they are being challenged with faith and discipline – practiced humbly but unapologetically. For Peggy it is especially joyful – she's happy to have their church experience again supporting the standards they want in their home. And she feels her battery recharge every week in the reverent, selfless atmosphere of the traditional Mass.

---

28 There were a number of priests who, acting independently, rode this informal "circuit." One of them who offered Mass at Peggy's home was a Father Carl Pulvermacher, who would surface again later in Peggy's journey.

All of this was made possible by a La Salette priest with a life-long passion for the Traditional Latin Mass, who had secured approval from his superior at the Mission parish to say one Latin Mass each Sunday.[29] The Mission's main chapel had even been renovated to add an intimate side altar suitable for his Latin Mass. The Mass itself was not publicized, and the church was relatively secluded, so attendance was modest. But Peggy was elated to fill one pew with her family every Sunday. This Mass was their home for about a year, and Peggy regarded the priest very highly. He became her confessor and would remain a lifelong friend of the family.

The La Salette campus vanished from Peggy's windshield. It was replaced by a church closer to home - the Church of the Immaculate Conception –a historic Lithuanian parish in East St. Louis, Illinois.[30] Word-of-mouth had delivered for her again; the Latin Mass was being offered by the pastor there, a Father Jonas (John) Gasiunas.

Immaculate Conception Church - Exterior

---

29 It was reported that the priest, in response to Vatican II, vowed to the Blessed Virgin that as long as he was a priest, she would have at least one priest (him) offering the Traditional Latin Mass.

30 Immaculate Conception Parish was actually located in the Diocese of Belleville (Illinois).

Immaculate Conception Church - Interior

The church was actually in another state, but it was conveniently located just across the river from downtown, so the Muehlemanns opted to give it a try. While proximity was a plus, there were other considerations. About that time, East Saint Louis had begun a decline (its population eventually reduced from 80,000 to 20,000 over several decades). Safety in the area was already a growing concern. All things considered, in 1974 crossing the river from Missouri to the Church of the Immaculate Conception for Sunday Mass could seem a peculiar idea to some. But Father Gasiunas was indeed drawing people. Peggy Muehlemann and her family were among them. In fact, the Meuhlemann clan (with five young sons) was a welcome addition to the parish. Churchgoers in this neighborhood were almost all elderly. This meant a shortage of young men to serve Mass, especially given the demanding nature of the server role in the Latin Rite. Peggy's boys had learned to serve Mass years ago from their mother and the travelling priests, and they jumped right in.

Thus a small contingent of hardy souls from Missouri found a church where their faith felt both familiar and exalted. If only it could last. Father Gasiunas was approaching 70 years old, though he appeared in good health. The number of faithful in his pews was small by diocesan standards, but growing a bit. Maybe someone at the Belleville diocesan office noticed an emerging popularity at this "outlier" parish, or maybe the parish was simply due for routine transition. In any event, less than a year after the Muehlemanns began their weekly pilgrimage across the river, a new young priest, Father Jean Paul Long, was assigned to Immaculate Conception Parish. Officially, he was there to relieve an aging pastor. The younger priest wielded authority and soon converted Masses from Traditional Latin to the Novus Ordo. Father Gasiunas complied, though reluctantly and with a bit of respectful resistance.[31] The esteemed elder priest who had first come to Immaculate Conception as associate pastor in 1953 was soon "re-assigned" to other duties elsewhere in the diocese.[32]

Meuhlemann membership at the splendid Lithuanian church came to an abrupt end. Returning to the La Sallette campus was not an option due to new restrictions on public use of their chapel. The family was yet again without a church. So they prayed. And Peggy plied her network. Late 1974 was a dark time for a tradition-loving Catholic in St. Louis. The spirit of Vatican II had a firm grip on the Church throughout the area. There was no indication that even one local priest would any longer publicly embrace traditional practices, including the Latin Rite. Thankfully, Peggy's word-of-mouth network still had connections.

The Muehlemanns resorted again to private Latin Masses at homes whenever they could be found. Peggy had been to Mass at the home of one friend more than once, and was intrigued by her host's approach. Her friend would drive to the airport to pick up a traveling priest who had been asked not to wear his collar. Upon arriving at her home, she shielded the priest and his items as they entered the home. The same was done later when they left the home. No more than ten people attended, and they were chosen from a carefully selected list. As it turns out, her friend was dreadfully afraid that neighbors (or anyone else) would frown upon her keeping company with

---

31 One of his signature acts of rebellion was to secretly swap out the new missals in the church with old missals. His gestures – and his general objection to changes at the Church – delighted his longtime parishioners.

32 It is unclear where (or whether) Father Gasiunas continued in a pastoral role after this re-assignment. Files at the Diocese of Belleville indicate he died in 1998 at age 94.

priests considered by many to be "renegades" from the Catholic Church. The priest who had been coming to St. Louis for her Masses was Father Hector Bolduc, a priest of the Society of St. Pius X (SSPX). Everything Peggy had seen so far suggested the priest was solidly orthodox. The Latin Masses had been just as she believed they should be. Peggy was comfortable, so her friend's secrecy struck her as unnecessary. It was perfect timing after Mass one evening when Peggy and Father Bolduc got to chatting. He shared that he wanted to reach out further in St. Louis, make the Mass available to more people and not secretive. Well, that was all Peggy needed to hear.

This memory brings a new image blazing across the van's ample windshield, but it wasn't another church. The new scene was unmistakably residential. Modest but comfortable, clean and fairly well lit, at least for an underground room. The home of the Muehlemann family - lower level to be exact - was now hosting the SSPX Latin Mass in St. Louis. It still wasn't on a regular schedule, but Father Bolduc offered a reverent low mass at their makeshift altar whenever travel allowed for a stop in St. Louis. Peggy got the word out every time and rsvp's were accepted until the room was full.

Though the Muehlemann basement operation was an expansion, it still seemed a safe bet that more Catholics in the area desired the Latin Mass. Father Bolduc wanted to serve this need. Peggy searched for a venue larger than her basement. By mid-1975 the duo had it figured out. The Latin Mass in St. Louis would move to a rented conference room at the Holiday Inn hotel. Father Bolduc would continue bringing the sacred items needed for the Mass. Peggy and the boys would bring the altar and other supplies.

And so, one last picture appeared to Peggy as she neared home on this Thanksgiving evening in 1975. The image was very fresh in her mind - the makeshift conference room chapel they had left just thirty minutes ago. Their hotel Mass was reasonably established now. Word-of-mouth was producing new faces. It seemed a dream coming true for so many desperate Catholics. Filled with warmth and optimism, she guided the van through one last right turn into her driveway. "Get it all unloaded, boys!"

PRIESTLY EMBER

The Meuhlemann boys knew the drill and commenced to unloading the van. On this night there was also a familiar guest in the van, who stepped out and quickly tended his own bags. Father Hector Bolduc had flown into town earlier in the day, just in time to arrive at the hotel for Mass. He was always invited to lodge at the Meuhlemann home when in town, an arrangement that guaranteed at least two home-cooked meals. These short home visits were a joy for Father Bolduc, whose busy travel schedule left scant time for getting to know the many traditional Catholic families he was now helping. Thanks to these visits, the Meuhlemanns also had the opportunity to learn a lot about this very special priest.

Just a year earlier, Father Hector Bolduc had been ordained in Econe, Switzerland by the founder of SSPX, Archbishop Marcel Lefebvre. Father Bolduc was 38 years old at the time and had already led a rather remarkable life. He was born in 1936 in Gilford, New Hampshire and served time in the U.S. Army as part of the occupation forces in Germany after World War II. He traveled extensively in the military and afterward, before joining the seminary in his early 20s. Even during seminary he continued his travels and studied the Illuminated Coptic Manuscripts in Ethiopia and the mosaics at the Hegia Sophia in what was once Constantinople. He was also a member of the Marians of the Immaculate Conception, first in Stockbridge, MA and later at Catholic University in Washington, D.C.

Hector Bolduc became an Ember because of the implementation of Vatican II. He could not bear to see the loss of the Tridentine (Latin) Mass, and he resolved to join the clergy. "That is what really galvanized me," said Bolduc. "I knew I had to get in there and protect it." Immediately after his ordination in June of 1974, Father Bolduc returned to the United States to support SSPX mission chapels all over the United States and assist SSPX's U.S. District Superior with the Society's newly founded seminary in Armada, Michigan.

His far-flung mission was in high gear by Thanksgiving of 1975. But tonight a warm turkey sandwich, a good night's rest at the Muehlemann's, and an early ride to the airport in the morning was all he asked.

NEW ROUTINE

Back in Belleville and soon after the dust settled from the Thanksgiving Mass, Mary and Judy arranged to meet. Judy knew she'd been stingy with details about the Mass when inviting Mary. It was time to fill in the blanks, in Mary's dining room and with the help of some sweetened iced tea. Mary heard for the first time extensive details about Archbishop Marcel Lefebvre and his Society of priests, their expansion to the United States, and their very recent arrival in St. Louis. The story was fascinating, full of conviction and courage. Mary was inspired. The backstory seemed to validate what she'd seen and felt on Thanksgiving evening. She was on alert for warning signs, but heard nothing troubling. Actually, certain critical facts about SSPX were more convincing than she had dared dream: Archbishop Lefebvre was a Bishop in good standing, he'd led a long and successful missionary apostolate in Africa, he had actually participated in Vatican II (and so shouldn't be considered an outsider), and the Society was unflinchingly devoted to the Traditional Latin Mass.

Mary was comfortable that the Mass she'd attended on Thanksgiving was the long-sought Mass of her childhood. Initial signs indicated that Marcel Lefebvre and SSPX were legitimate. And in 1975 she also still held hope that the Belleville Diocese (and St. Mary's Church in particular) would reverse course back toward tradition. So she went to Sunday Mass at St. Mary's (despite it being more difficult to tolerate) and drove to St. Louis (usually by herself) whenever word arrived of an SSPX priest visit. For the time being, that was the best approach available for satisfying her highest priority: to worship and receive God, as regularly and as devoutly as possible, at the Holy Sacrifice of the Mass.

BACK TO THE BOOKS

Life for Mary was finding a steadier pace. Only three kids still lived at home, giving her a little well-deserved breathing room on the child-rearing front. Her new Mass routine wasn't perfect but it did at least provide stability. Sunday Mass at St. Mary's was increasingly unbearable, but at least for now - for the first time in many years - she didn't feel a need to scour the earth for answers and new options.

Labor Day 1976 arrived with the opportunity to enjoy a gorgeous afternoon with their good friends Louie and Jeanne who had invited Mary, Russ and their two boys out for a boat ride on the Kaskaskia River just 20 miles east of town. With everyone enjoying the sunshine, Louie steered the small boat up and down the river. To varying levels of success, most of the group had taken their turns behind the boat on water skis. As talk of returning to shore began, a freak and fateful event took place. Crossing over the wake of a passing boat caused a short airborne thrill, an experience they had enjoyed several times earlier in the day. But this particular lift had a profound repercussion as Mary, situated in the rear of the boat, landed awkwardly and hard. Following an excruciating van ride to the hospital, the diagnosis of a broken back would result in a 2-week hospital stay and 6 months of immobile bed rest in a tight, rigid brace.

It was a memorable stay at Belleville's Catholic hospital for the 47-year old mother. Pain killing medicines notwithstanding, on the first day of her stay, Mary noticed that facing her from the wall across the room was a figure of the risen Lord. She'd expected to see a crucifix, an icon that could help her join her current suffering to Christ's. She asked her attending nurse about the figure. The only answer given was that traditional crucifixes had been removed from all rooms.[33]

---

[33] Mary wished in hindsight that she'd asked (or demanded) a traditional crucifix in her room, but she hadn't felt it her place to make the request at the time. Later, she spoke to a friend (Mrs. Biver) who had been in the same hospital and HAD requested a crucifix. The nun caring for her actually brought one of her own crucifixes and placed it on the wall in Mrs. Biver's room. For this kind gesture the nun was eventually reprimanded by her superior.

A priest, the hospital chaplain, was making the rounds the next morning and stepped into her room. Always eager to hear from a member of the clergy about church matters, Mary engaged him in a discussion that eventually honed in on the status of the Traditional Latin Mass. Her simple question was, "Can we have the Latin Mass?" The priest explained that the Old Mass had been replaced by the New Mass, and said he would lend her a book that would help her understand. Later in the day he returned with a copy of Christ Among Us by Anthony Wilhelm. True to form and with plenty of time to read, Mary immersed herself in the book. She saw right away that there was much to note in the book and she had highlighters brought from home. Over two days, she identified many areas of concern with the book, but arrived at one general thought encompassing much of the trouble; on a variety of issues Mr. Wilhelm stated that official Catholic teaching ought to be considered an ideal, but not a standard that Catholics could realistically achieve. Mary looked forward to hearing the hospital chaplain's explanations for such positions. Just a day later the chaplain re-entered her room ready to see whether his student had drawn anything from the book. Mary began to point out numerous captions she'd highlighted because they seemed to contradict what she'd been taught. Without any discussion, the priest suddenly and unexpectedly turned and stormed out of the room, slamming the door shut. Seconds later a nurse rushed in, frantic to know what had caused the commotion. The priest never returned to collect his loaned book.[34]

The encounters with the hospital chaplain supercharged Mary's ambition to understand what was happening within the Catholic Church, and specifically why the TLM had become such an unspeakable topic. Her previous study of the Vatican II documents had shown that the Council Fathers considered the Latin Rite important and relevant, something to be protected and encouraged. She wondered if Pope John XXIII himself, instigator of the

---

34 In the years after Vatican II, Christ Among Us was the most widely used introduction to Catholicism in the United States. The book had many critics, Catholics United for the Faith being among the most vocal. In 1984, Joseph Cardinal Ratzinger, at the time head of the Vatican's Sacred Congregation for the Doctrine of the Faith, ordered Archbishop Peter L. Gerety of Newark, NJ to remove his imprimatur. The Vatican said only that the book was "not suitable as a Catholic text". (NYT 11/29/84)

Council, might have privately wished to scuttle the TLM. Ready to investigate that possibility, Mary contacted her cousin Ethel, a delightful lady and librarian at East St. Louis High School.[35] What Mary needed right now was information about Pope John XXIII. Ethel's immediate recommendation was the Pope's autobiography Journal of a Soul and she was quick to produce the book. It became Mary's first undertaking as she started her 6 months of bed confinement at home. Happily for Mary, the project yielded a clear answer. Pope John XXIII's autobiography reaffirmed that he dearly loved the Traditional Latin Mass. It was unthinkable that this pope would have wanted it changed. Then again, this meant Mary had driven into another dead end. The question remained, "Why did they change the Mass?"

---

35   She also helped at the Belleville Public Library. A brilliant and engaging lady with remarkable recall, Ethel knew books and she knew where to find them. She also knew a lot of people, so if she didn't know something or which book to consult - she knew somebody who did.

CHAPTER 5:
PEACE + PERIL

Finally back on her feet and with a tolerable worship routine (Sunday Mass at St. Mary's and periodic weekday evening TLM in St. Louis), Mary's top personal priority in 1977 shifted to the search for a permanent place of worship where she could be fully at peace. SSPX offered some real hope, but - in addition to being distant in St. Louis - their operation was still young, had no permanent infrastructure, and couldn't even offer Sunday Mass. Things were no better in Belleville where the diocese continued evolving away from her understanding of the Catholic Church.

Mary continued praying and researching. By now she realized she'd likely confront more dilemmas along the way, but had no way of knowing what they might be.

GATHERING LITERATURE

To appreciate the scope of Mary's research one needs to know just a little about the most interesting feature of her home ... her collection of faith-based books. It started shortly after the broken back recuperation, when the woman hungry for information teamed with the energetic librarian, sparking Mary and Ethel's great book adventure. Ethel called Mary one day to ask whether she might be interested in buying a full set of Catholic Encyclopedias Ethel had just seen at a Belleville Library book sale. At ten dollars, it was a deal Mary couldn't pass up. When Mary expressed interest in other book sales in the area, Ethel quickly uncovered the wider world of public book sales. As is still customary in some areas, sales of donated books were held periodically to benefit worthy causes. Two popular sales occurring annually in the late 1970's were at Memorial Hospital in West Belleville and at Famous Barr department store in St. Louis County. Mountains of used books were available for sale at bargain basement prices, stacked on endless tables under tents in large parking lots. Diverse crowds swarmed the multi-day sales, everyone seeking great finds in certain subject areas or by favorite authors. Mary was laser-focused on books about the Catholic faith, in particular those published before 1960. The pickings were surprisingly excellent – and there was good reason for this. At this time, virtually every Catholic organization or entity was throwing out its "old" books.[36] Curiously, the purge seemed especially rich in books about the Saints of the Church. Mary always arrived at a sale with twenty dollars in her pocket. She always left with a treasure trove and money to spare. The great book adventure carried on for five years.

At home, the collection ultimately spread from her living room into her spacious basement, and included thousands of books. When she and Russ eventually downsized, she agreed to prune the collection and less than half the collection made the trip to their new, smaller home. Today some 1,100 books remain. Topics cover almost everything imaginable including Church history, classics, biographies, councils, devotions, ecumenism, miracles, heresies, Christ, the Blessed Virgin Mary, Protestantism and other faiths, the Mass, meditations, Doctors of the Church, Popes, religious orders, theology, and more - especially the Saints. Mary hasn't read all of the books, but she has read most – some several times. Her highlights and comments mark the pages. Summaries of many of the books, most painstakingly banged out on the tool of the day (a manual Smith Corona typewriter), remain neatly organized in a row of mismatched filing cabinets.[37]

---

36 It seemed every source possible was contributing, especially grade schools, high schools, and seminaries - ownership easily known from stamps in the books. Rare finds included Priests' Missals (used for Mass) and Martyrologies.

37 The entire library is catalogued, detailing the specifics of each book from topic and author to number of pages and copyright date. Most important in Mary's view is the classification assigned to each book. There are only three classifications: primary, secondary, and giveaway. Her wish for her children is that they read every book she has indicated as

SUNDAY MASS: EVERY EMBER'S DILEMMA

The worship routine Mary had initiated just after Thanksgiving in 1975 was still her operating mode in 1977; Sunday Mass at St. Mary's and periodic Thursday evening TLM in St. Louis. This regimen might even have sustained her well beyond 1977, but (as recounted earlier) in that year St. Mary's Church began to allow, and in fact encouraged, communion-in-the-hand. That "innovation" changed everything. Mary now faced a major dilemma. Should she continue attending Sunday Mass at St. Mary's, feeling - as she did - that the sacrament of Communion and the Holy Mass itself were somehow being violated or even desecrated? She saw two alternatives.

1. Attend Sunday Novus Ordo Mass at St. Mary's, or

2. Do not go to Mass at all on Sunday, because the only available Mass was the Novus Ordo.

Research provided a lot to think about. A strong argument seemed to flow from the historical experiences of Catholics under times of persecution. Mary was particularly moved by Saint John Vianney who, with his devout parents and his siblings, endured the cruel persecution of faithful Catholics meted out in the French Revolution.[38] When it became clear to the Vianney family that the "new" Sunday Mass imposed on them was no longer the Catholic Mass, they immediately ceased to attend the parish church.[39]

Mary absorbed all information she could get her hands on, and then deliberated with a lot of prayer. She was not comfortable with skipping Sunday Mass altogether, and settled on a compromise. She would continue

primary, which is a very exclusive group of books she feels are fundamental to knowing the Catholic faith. Secondary books she recommends as worthwhile, if one has an interest in the topic. Giveaways are earmarked for charitable causes in time. The library itself will be inherited by one of her children for maintenance and sharing.

38 Saint Father John Vianney, also known worldwide as the Curé d'Ars. His family lived in the countryside village of Dardilly, where traditional faith was held firmly. Their local parish had been assigned to a new and heretical priest, one who had signed the Obligatory Oath swearing loyalty to the state. Ref: The Curé d'Ars, Chapter 2, by Abbe Francis Trochu (1927/1949)

39 After leaving their parish church the Vianney family attached to the underground church where Mass was offered in secrecy and sporadically by faithful Catholic priests who traveled in hiding, marked for beheading if they were caught by state authorities.

to attend St. Mary's for Sunday Mass, but would no longer take Communion. It satisfied the Sunday obligation as she understood it, and enabled her to avoid participating in what she considered a sacrilege. She prayed that God might accept it as her best and most reverent option. It must be noted that for a true believer in the infinite grace bestowed by the Holy Eucharist, declining Communion is a heart-breaking sacrifice. Sunday without the Holy Eucharist was distressful for an Ember. For the record, Mary's decision at the time took into account one other factor. She and Russ wanted to continue the example of attending Sunday Mass for her two youngest children still at home. Her compromise approach did set the example, but she cried and prayed a lot when the others weren't around.

Embers arrived at moments of decision regarding their Sunday Mass dilemma whenever their unique personal journeys forced it on them. And in the angst of those moments, because communications in the 1970's were so relatively "primitive," they seldom had the benefit of knowing their fellow Embers or how those fellow Embers had themselves reasoned through the dilemma. Recall that Peggy Muehlemann opted out of Sunday Mass very quickly after the New Mass was introduced in 1969. To her, the Novus Ordo Mass seemed offensive to God.

Uninvited and fraught with peril, the Sunday Mass dilemma was a perpetual stalker of an Ember.

PROMISING PATH / TREACHEROUS FOOTING

SSPX's presence in St. Louis was limited in 1976. It was a tiny community with a low profile, not easy to find even for those searching for something like it. Mary felt fortunate to have discovered it. For her, the Society held promise and it was time to step forward on that path. At the same time, she wasn't blind to the possibility of treacherous footing ahead. A two-fold approach seemed prudent, a sort of trust-but-verify policy. First, she gave high priority to attending SSPX Masses in St. Louis. But second, she would continue her research to learn everything possible about Archbishop Lefebvre and his Society.

That research quickly uncovered major concerns. Since the founding of SSPX in 1970, the Archbishop and SSPX had been in good standing with the Roman Catholic Church and with the Pope. That took a turn in 1975 when hostile attitudes toward the Society came to the fore in Rome. Recognition of SSPX as a canonical organization was lifted. Then in 1976 the Archbishop was charged by Rome with ordaining priests without Vatican approval and with praying the "banned" Tridentine Mass. Pope Paul VI formally suspended Lefebvre for an indefinite time from exercising almost all Sacraments, specifically Holy Orders. For his part, Archbishop Lefebvre maintained that his suspension was not legally valid because he was never given opportunity to present his side. "They have better legal defense in the Soviet Union," the Archbishop declared at the time.

Such was the conflict raging between SSPX and the Vatican at the very time Mary was getting acquainted with SSPX. It is hard to imagine how a lifelong Catholic, raised to revere the Vatican and the Pope, might even consider not deferring to their authority and simply steer clear of SSPX. But our Mary was stubborn; a researcher, a thinker, a devout believer. And she prayed relentlessly. In this instance, among all the arguments, one document loomed large. It was the Profession of Faith delivered as a sermon by Archbishop Lefebvre on the day of the ordinations in question - June 29, 1976. It was thunderous in rebuking Vatican II's Modernist actions and in defending both tradition in the Catholic Church and the Mass of All Time.[40] A copy of the sermon had been swiftly distributed worldwide at SSPX Masses. Mary

---

40 Apologia Pro Marcel Lefebvre, Volume 1, Chapter 11, The Ordinations of 29 June 1976. Positions on which Archbishop Lefebvre expounded: 1) the Protestant notion of the Mass is being introduced into the Holy Church, 2) the fundamental and gravely wrong mentality of modern man is that power (authority) lies with the assembly and not in God, 3) the New Mass is democratic rather than hierarchical and thus a whole new ideology, 4) priestly ordination bestows on an individual a character above the people of God, 5) the Vatican now errs in accepting the plurality of religions and no longer accepting the Social Kingship of Our Lord Jesus Christ, and 6) priests are assured by virtue of Saint Pius V's Bull that the Old Mass may be said in perpetuity without fear of censure.

weighed her various findings[41] and entertained arguments from all sides. And she prayed. In the end, she believed God's one true Church couldn't possibly deny the legitimacy of the priests ordained by Archbishop Lefebvre in 1976. So she resolved to continue down the path with SSPX for now. It was yet another gut-wrenching decision for an Ember.

On the ground with SSPX in St. Louis, all seemed positive. Thursday evening Mass continued to attract new "parishioners." Again, larger quarters were needed. This time Peggy found affordable space for the SSPX Thursday evening mass in the Clara Hempelmann office building in St. Louis' history-rich neighborhood of Princeton Heights.

Clara Hempelmann office building at 6819 Gravois Avenue.

---

41   Among the many sources of information Mary studied, another influential one was Newman's Apologia Pro Vita Sua.

The location was central, well-suited for people driving from almost any corner of the St. Louis area. The fact they were in a basement didn't deter these stalwart mass-goers – they'd been there before. What mattered was the opportunity to worship at their beloved Traditional Latin Mass. For three years the faithful arrived on Thursday evenings with Missals in hand, most lugging makeshift kneeling pads. They parked on the street, ambled to the shiny front doors, proceeded into the lobby, then down the stairs and into the rows of folding chairs. Low Mass was offered at the Muehlemann's makeshift altar. And their number continued to grow.

SSPX Mass in the basement of Clara Hempelmann Building

Thursday evenings, 1977-1979

PERMANENT HOME

By 1979 the Thursday night crowd was bulging up against the basement walls at Clara Hempelmann.[42] The need for larger, more permanent facilities and

---

42 St. Louis was not alone in this experience. Similar steady growth had been experienced at SSPX missions throughout the U.S. and in other countries. Archbishop Lefebvre and his team of leaders focused on a future where it may be necessary for their Society to be freestanding financially and administratively, although they continued to seek unqualified reunion with the Vatican. Two pillars of their future plan were seminaries and mission facilities. First priority for SSPX would always be the training of new priests. A U.S. seminary had been opened and was operating in Armada, Michigan. Plans were underway to expand and move the seminary to Connecticut. For decades to come the constraining factor on the Society's reach would be the capacity in its seminaries. The society has never wanted for

added personnel was certainly clear. Father Bolduc and others would prove themselves very capable in accomplishing this.[43]

Father Bolduc enlisted Peggy to search for yet another new location for their St. Louis Masses. This time SSPX hoped to find an actual church, perhaps even a property with potential to serve eventually as a "parish" that would include a school. In short order she found an interesting opportunity. About fifteen minutes west of their current gathering place, the former Grant public school was on the auction block. It was a grade school building, and there was no church. But there was a gym/auditorium with a stage. And the three and one-half acre lot included enough greenspace for a church to eventually be built. The vision appealed to Father Bolduc and he authorized an agent to bid for it. A bid of $200,000 was deemed appropriate. So, to best any other bidder thinking the same, Father Bolduc's representative (The Friends of the Society of St. Pius X) submitted a bid of $205,000. To their dismay, a competitor bid $205,050. The school district declared SSPX's competitor the high responsive bidder. The SSPX team was devastated. They returned to the real estate drawing board, and prayed they could quickly find another suitable opportunity. Sometimes Providence seems a fitting explanation for the course of events, and this may have been one of those times. Weeks later, the phone rang. The school district was calling to inform The Friends of the Society of St. Pius X that the high bidder was insisting on renovations and repairs to the facility prior to closing on the deal. If the Society still wanted the property and was willing to accept it "as is," then it was theirs. In short order the Society answered, "Yes." The deal went through.[44]

---

vocations, only for more of the qualified teachers and suitable facilities to ensure careful selection and thorough training of the young men.

43   Finances were, of course, a constant factor. The faithful were passionate and as generous as possible in their support of this orthodox movement. Some wealthy benefactors were among them. SSPX was by no means a wealthy organization, but they did have at least some resources with which to plan and execute ongoing growth.

44   One more sidebar on Providence .... The next December, still year one of owning the property, a faithful parishioner Dr. Dean Bauer, contacted the Church. He was going to sell some stocks prior to year's end, and wished to use the proceeds to pay off the mortgage on the Church's property. This deal also went through.

Having completed the purchase of the property, all that stood between SSPX and their first mass in the new auditorium was an occupancy permit. This process became a bit more contentious than usual as word spread locally that SSPX had purchased the property. A small but vocal group of city residents, opposed to SSPX for reasons fully known only to them, placed as much pressure as possible on the permitting authorities to turn the Society away. As it turns out, the only compliance issue that could be found by the inspectors was a shortfall of parking at the facility. This could have forced SSPX to either walk away or spend money to add parking while delaying their move-in. The dilemma was settled quickly when management at the insurance company located across Grant Road stepped forward to graciously offer the use of their parking lot to parishioners attending Sunday Mass at the chapel. [45]

The obstacles had been overcome and SSPX was officially putting down roots in St. Louis.[46] Queen of the Holy Rosary Church held its first Traditional Latin Mass in the modified auditorium on a Sunday in late 1979. For most in attendance, it was the first Sunday Latin Mass in almost ten years. Embers glowed on that day like never before.

DRAWING FIRE

In the process of creating Queen of the Holy Rosary, the parishioners had faced slings and arrows from the general public. This had been a little surprising and a little painful, but it was behind them. Unfortunately, they also now suspected that more fights lay ahead.

An event of major significance was scheduled for May of 1980. Archbishop Marcel Lefebvre, who hadn't travelled to the United States in over five years, was scheduled to personally consecrate their new chapel.

---

45 SSPX encountered the same kind of resistance around the U.S., for example in Kansas City, New York, and Texas.

46 Queen of the Holy Rosary Academy opened for K-5 classes the following year and later added grades 6-8. The opening of the school also met with resistance from the local community. A tussle over formal accreditation was finally settled after a full presentation of the school's curriculum to city and state panels.

Visits by the Archbishop were drawing the attention of the local diocese and the local press wherever he went, due to the rising profile of the Society worldwide. St. Louis was no exception. In advance of Lefebvre's visit, John L. May, Archbishop of St. Louis, launched the following attack on SSPX in the city's most prominent newspaper:

> *"No Catholic may support in any way this tragic movement by Archbishop Lefebvre. I regret very much his coming to St. Louis because of the disunity he represents. I call upon Catholics at this time to reaffirm our loyalty and allegiance to our Holy Father, Pope John Paul II, by ignoring this visit and this chapel."*[47]

For over five years SSPX had operated quietly in St. Louis, unbeknownst to most Catholics. Their new chapel and the visit of Archbishop Lefebvre changed all that. Tension between the Diocesan Church and SSPX was now out in the open. And it was unlikely to subside any time soon.[48] Catholics throughout the diocese heard Archbishop May's messages and from them formed opinions about SSPX and Queen of the Holy Rosary chapel. As if Embers like Mary didn't have enough personal stress already, they would now be incurring disdain from other Catholics in the St. Louis area.

Public pressure and all, Queen of the Holy Rosary Chapel was a game-changer for Mary. Her personal Sunday Mass dilemma was solved. For years to come, a satisfying new routine took hold. Russ attended Sunday Mass at St. Mary's in Belleville and Mary drove to St. Louis.

---

47 St. Louis Post Dispatch, May 18, 1980

48 Father Bolduc fired back at Archbishop May in September 1980, sarcastically pointing to eight of May's most controversial accomplishments in his first year as Archbishop. The blistering one-page statement ended "Yes, St. Louis, you do have a new bishop. The question is – is he Catholic"? MAYbe he is but MAYbe he isn't." (ref: "Saint Louis Gets a New Bishop", Hector Bolduc September 1980). Eight years later, by publishing notice in his St. Louis Review that the Faithful " … are going to have to make their choice now," Archbishop May elicited in response an illuminating comparison from Francois Laisney, Superior of SSXP in New Zealand. Among various factors, Laisney suggests the faithful will hold May accountable for "presiding over the decomposition of the Catholic Church in America," wherein "the past twenty years the diocese of St. Louis has lost more than 85% of the number of seminarians it had, more than 40% of the Catholic students, and almost 70% of its teaching nuns!" … whereas SSPX has opened six new seminaries and many convents. " (Angelus Magazine - June 1988)

FOR BETTER AND FOR WORSE

So Mary and Russ went their own ways for Sunday Mass starting in 1979. This arrangement might seem odd or difficult. It was. But it was understandable. For over ten years their Catholic faith, Sunday Mass in particular, had been a constant sore spot. They'd experienced different feelings about changes in the Church, Mass, and even parish life since the mid-1960's. They were frequently at odds about how (and whether) to accept changes, both personally and as a family. Russ' default position was to obey the direction of his Diocesan parish priest. "If my priest is wrong, then he'll pay the price, not me." Mary would have liked to do the same, but as we know often could not. Certain lines were drawn. For instance Russ always insisted that "the boys" go with him to Mass. Mary always deferred to Russ where he insisted. For his part, Russ was generally agreeable to Mary seeking out her own preferences. They had found workable compromises over the years but it was never without tension. Now they had a routine that met everyone's needs, though nobody would ever suggest it was ideal.

Stories of other couples who didn't see eye-to-eye on their Catholic faiths at the time were as common as Stag beer at the corner tavern. Mary's close friend and dearest fellow Ember was a perfect example. Her name was Mary Ann and her husband went by the nickname Smitty. Both were Catholics. They had lived in Belleville and been long-time members of St. Teresa Parish where their kids had gone to school. Once those school years were over, Mary Ann and Smitty were free to follow their dream. They bought property outside Mascoutah, Illinois about fifteen miles east of Belleville, built a home alongside its small lake, and settled in to tend the property and entertain grandkids. Kind and generous, they made fast friends at their new local Catholic parish, Holy Childhood Church. Things were steady and predictable for them until the Vatican II tidal wave rolled into Mascoutah and things started changing at Holy Childhood. Smitty wasn't fazed. He embraced his new role at Mass as Eucharistic Minister, and simply felt (like the vast majority) that "a Catholic just needs to be obedient and go along with whatever the Church says." Mary Ann abhorred the changes. In fact, her plight and her personal angst were chillingly similar to Mary's through the 60's and 70's. Eventually Mary Ann would take to traveling to St. Louis for Sunday Latin Mass while Smitty stayed behind for Mass in Mascoutah. Their Mass dilemma kept them apart on most Sundays for years.

Peggy Muehlemann and her husband Ed were another variation of Ember marriage. Because he wasn't Catholic, Ed had very seldom attended Mass with her and the family. This hadn't changed even when Peggy found SSPX and their St. Louis Masses became more regular. Interestingly though, he *wanted* to share her faith, and worked for years to personally sort it out. Ed was always fully behind Peggy's efforts and eagerly chipped in wherever he could. Their marriage didn't suffer torment of differing convictions, though it was surely shaped by the endless hours Peggy devoted to the fledgling Chapel and school. Her efforts would fill a separate volume.[49]

Such were the married lives of Embers.

READING AND RIGHTING

At the outset of the 1980's no one knew how (or even if) the discord between the Catholic Church and SSPX could be resolved. Mary had chosen her path and had no reservations about the decisions she'd made so far. But she also presumed more twists lay ahead. She vowed to keep learning about SSPX and the Mass and history, and to stay informed of ongoing developments in the Church ... so that come what may, she could be confident in making decisions that were right for her. Fortunately, that kind of work was right in her wheelhouse - it mostly called for reading.

Books, magazines, and newspapers were the staples of research at the time. All three needed to be deployed. Of course she kept close tabs on The Messenger, Belleville's weekly diocesan paper. It provided Church news and commentary from all levels – Vatican, United States, and local diocese. From

---

49 Having already championed the startup of the St. Louis Mass through multiple locations with Father Bolduc, Peggy continued as a driving force behind both the chapel and the school at Queen of the Holy Rosary Academy, including service as the school's vice principal. Her fellow parishioners swear they've never known a harder worker or a more humble human being.

another viewpoint The Remnant was also on Mary's reading list. A well-known source of news and commentary for the traditionalist community, Mary saw her first copy of The Remnant on a table outside the Queen of the Holy Rosary chapel. And of course there were other periodicals. Clippings from Columbia Magazine by the Knights of Columbus, for instance, were common in her stack.

True to form, Mary continued to read books. Many came straight off the shelves of her home library as she continued to delve deeper into Church history and into specific topics like the Mass. Newer books, if they promised to be worthwhile, would be borrowed from the library or maybe purchased at a bookstore, though her budget for book purchases was pretty meager. The works of one author seemed to stand out among the rest. Mary first came across Michael Davies in The Remnant where his column Letter From London was always prominently featured. Davies was a British teacher and writer, raised Baptist but a convert to Catholicism while a student in the 1950s. This was a man of boundless energy, known worldwide in Catholic circles, one of the most prolific traditionalist apologists of his time, who eventually served twelve years as president of the international organization Una Voce. He'd initially been a supporter of Vatican II, but became critical of the liturgical changes that followed in its wake ... and along the way became a supporter of Archbishop Marcel Lefebvre. He saw SSPX as an important organization and produced a powerful three-volume series of books titled Apologia Pro Marcel Lefebvre in which he defended Lefebvre. Never had Mary so eagerly anticipated the release of a book as she did the first volume of this series by Davies in 1979. The gifted author did not disappoint and the books were foundational in Mary's research.[50]

Michael Davies was an Ember, which may or may not explain the following story of a remarkable and unlikely bond formed between the author from London and the housewife from Belleville, Illinois. In 1988,

---

50   Davies' Liturgical Revolution is another highly relevant, three-volume set. It includes Cranmer's Godly Order, Pope John's Council, and Pope Paul's New Mass

Mary typed a letter to "Mr. Davies" to comment on his latest Letter From London column. She introduced herself as a fan of many years who "holds as one of my treasured possessions a copy of Apologia Pro Marcel Lefebvre that you autographed for me in St. Mary's Kansas" nine years prior. She continued, "Your many books and pamphlets have helped me understand the things I had previously just felt in my heart." She then unceremoniously launched three paragraphs of criticism asserting that in his article he seemed to lose all sense of humility, contradicted himself, and deserted Archbishop Lefebvre. She closed with "I cringe at my audacity to write you in such a manner, but you did invite your readers to send their comments ..." One might expect a busy and renowned author to ignore the input. Yet barely two weeks passed before a blue air mail envelope arrived from Cromwell Avenue in London. In two articulate hand-written pages Davies thanked her for the "interesting letter," reminisced about the wonderful hope-filled weekend all had spent at St. Mary's, apologized for any confusion stemming from his recent article (the result, he said, of trying to impartially synthesize large amounts of material), invited Mary to detail her objections more specifically (promising to clarify in a subsequent Remnant issue), reaffirmed his high regard for Lefebvre (with whom he is on good terms, corresponds regularly, and maintains an open invitation to Econe), talked of his multiple "apropos" comments to both the Pope and to Lefebvre defending - as characteristic of true friendship and loyalty - the Archbishop's criticism of what he believed to be the Pope's mistakes (while likening it to Mary's "courtesy" in pointing out what she considered to be Davies' own mistakes), clarified where he specifically disagrees with Lefebvre, and - in closing - kindly expressed hope that he might meet her again one day.

Weeks later Mary replied with abundant thanks, withdrawing her accusation of a lack of humility on his part. And, as invited, she went on to detail her questions about Davies' previous article, most of them apparent inconsistencies between the recent article and his earlier book Apologia. The specific matters were wide-ranging, from Lefebvre's tangle with the Vatican to the intricacies of Canon Law. She closed acknowledging their common perspectives and thanking him especially for his years of service to the Church. Davies replied again by hand, this time sharing his recent struggles with the flu and making his case for what he considered tactical mistakes by Lefebvre. He also humbly commented "I must say that I felt most embarrassed by your thorough knowledge of my books. You know them far better than I do." The two corresponded on and off for five years … pointed, scholarly, eloquent, and gracious … as "true friends" in Davies' parlance. Two Embers who never did meet again, but managed to enrich and support each other.

EPIC FORK IN THE ROAD

Through the early and mid-80's there was, so to speak, peace in the land. Everyone's "workable" Sunday Mass routine continued, and little happened within the Catholic Church or within SSPX to force anyone to re-consider.[51] SSPX continued its steady growth globally and in the United States. Queen of the Holy Rosary Church grew and became more established. The "spirit of Vatican II" continued to guide the Catholic Church worldwide despite declining metrics, carrying St. Mary's Church in Belleville and Holy Childhood in Mascoutah in tow.[52] But as the late 1980's approached, a tension began to build. At stake was the long-term viability of SSPX. SSPX is, first and foremost, a Society of priests. Since its origin, new priests had been trained at its seminaries and ordained by its Bishop (Archbishop) Marcel Lefebvre. He was the Society's one and only Bishop, and thus the only one able to ordain priests. Having been born in 1905, the Archbishop's age was a growing concern. If he were to pass away, it was quite possible that no

---

51 One minor exception was an indult issued in 1984 by the Vatican. In theory the action allowed for the possibility of Traditional Latin Masses being held anywhere in the world. However, the requirement that Masses be approved by the local bishop ultimately dampened any hope of widespread use of the Mass.

52 Locally, one noteworthy development did occur. The Archdiocese of St. Louis opened St. Agatha's Church in St. Louis proper. The establishment of this parish, committed to routinely offering the Traditional Latin Mass, was seen by most as an attempt to lure traditional Catholics away from the new SSPX parish at Queen of the Holy Rosary (a position strengthened by the fact that St. Agatha's was started in 1983, before Indult 1AND in contradiction of the Archdiocese's public stance regarding the Latin Mass at the time).

other bishop in the world would ordain SSPX priests going forward. This scenario would mean death to SSPX within a few decades, and in all likelihood this was the Vatican's preferred eventuality. Archbishop Lefebvre obviously did not want this to happen. He feared that continuity of the Church's sacred tradition depended on bishops following behind him. The faceoff between SSPX and the Vatican over this issue is well documented and need not be detailed here.[53] A summary of relevant facts includes: the Vatican and SSPX did discuss this matter for a long time and negotiations did take place between them; the parties could not arrive at terms that were mutually acceptable; Archbishop Lefebvre proceeded – against the expressed wishes of the Pope - to consecrate four new SSPX bishops on June 30, 1988; and following the consecrations, the Vatican, via Apostolic Letter Ecclesia Dei, declared Archbishop Lefebvre and the four new Bishops had incurred automatic excommunication from the Church.

The relevant question here is … What did this mean to an Ember?

This was a major event for traditional Catholics. It had potential to greatly increase the angst of Latin Mass-goers, most of whom had already paid a high price for a long time. Followers of SSPX (including the existing priests) would now have to decide whether to (a) return to the Diocesan Churches and be in "full communion" with Rome, where they fully expected to be miserable or (b) continue in the Society and bear whatever level of anxiety they might feel over the Vatican's statements regarding excommunication. To heighten the stakes, the Pope included a sweetener in his letter Ecclesia Dei. Making no secret of its intention to reclaim the faithful from SSPX pews, the letter encouraged Bishops to open their dioceses to more Latin Masses (called the Extraordinary Form of the Mass). He also soon initiated the Church's own Latin Mass priestly society, The Priestly Fraternity of St. Peter (FSSP).

Some members of Queen of the Holy Rosary did eventually leave the parish over the 1988 consecrations. The situation caused enormous

---

53   Ref: https://en.wikipedia.org/wiki/%C3%89c%C3%B4ne_consecrations; Archbishop Lefebvre and the Vatican, 1987-1988, by Father Francois Laisney.

strain in some cases; one husband and wife (friends of Mary) divided on the issue. Even a few priests left SSPX, some of them helping to found FSSP. And even The Remnant, for years a supporter of SSPX, turned sour on Archbishop Lefebvre.

Mary approached it like she always did, with prayer and research. For starters, her past studies on Church history and on the Mass had increased her confidence and broadened her knowledge. She digested every fact she could obtain about the negotiations and the consecrations.[54] Through it all, she found nothing that caused her to doubt the path she was already on. In fact, she was strengthened by the effort.[55] She had tested the traditional Catholic faith on this matter as hard as she could, and it all added up. She would continue to follow Archbishop Lefebvre, who said to his followers before the consecrations, "I cannot leave you orphans." And she was at peace about it.

SHEPHERD EMBERS

The mere mention of Econe and consecrations calls to mind an especially precious type of Ember. They wear collars. Their numbers were infinitesimally small in the days after Vatican II, known because they were the few who took public action. Something inside them could not abide the Church's change in direction, so they did what they thought necessary. Some, for example, formed the SSPX and eventually recruited others. Priests from this group made possible the joy of parishioners at Queen of the Holy Rosary, then and now.

Father Hector Bolduc was certainly one of the Shepherd Embers. How he came to be an SSPX priest was discussed earlier. As one of the first SSPX priests in the United States, he serviced mission chapels across the country while he also assisted in running the Society's new seminary in Armada,

---

54 An important fact for Mary was that the Archbishop formally requested a trial, which he was never granted.

55 Including a new meditation over the Fifth Joyful Mystery where Jesus disobeyed man's rules in order to serve His Father.

Michigan. Father Bolduc, a tireless missionary who seldom slept more than three or four hours a night, worked a dizzying schedule. One look at a typical weekend in the late 1970's confirms this: Saturday afternoon departure from Dickinson, Texas flying to Wichita (on any other Saturday it might be Omaha or Springfield MO), shuttle from airport to location, celebrate Mass, reverse course and return to Dickinson for a late turn-in, Sunday morning Mass at 8:00 am at Queen of Angels Church in Dickinson, then fly to Kansas City for Mass at noon, followed by flight to St. Louis to celebrate Mass at 6:00 pm. At each of these mission locations he also heard confessions. Stringently following traditional rules for fasting, Father Bolduc refrained from eating after midnight Saturday, which explains his appreciation of the home cooking waiting at Muehlemann's on Sunday night.

In addition to his pastoral activity, Father Bolduc shouldered an ever-growing management role. The Society needed to build infrastructure and suitable churches were fast becoming a priority. Luckily for SSPX, the resourceful Father Bolduc proved very adept at this. As he had acquired Queen of the Holy Rosary Church in St. Louis, so he purchased the Society's complex at St. Mary's, Kansas and many other churches. Often the properties, such as Queen of the Angels in Dickinson and the cathedral-esque St. Vincent DePaul Church in Kansas City were purchased by intermediaries on behalf of the Society so that the local diocese would not be aware of the planned "crime" of celebrating the Traditional Latin Mass. And with few exceptions, the buildings needed a lot of work to be useable.

Father Bolduc left SSPX in 1983 to become an independent priest.[56] Officially, he returned to his home town of Gilford, New Hampshire, moving into his boyhood home on their working farm. In reality, he serviced chapels in numerous states including Wisconsin, Ohio, and Michigan.[57] He devoted a great deal of time to St. Michael's Church in De Pere Wisconsin, functioning

---

56 The headstrong Father Bolduc and SSPX couldn't resolve conflicting views on certain matters that were never made public. It was an amicable split, and both parties remained respectful of the other in the years that followed.

57 Father Bolduc had nine siblings. His brothers cared for the farm (including the buffalo) while he was away at other chapels.

as pastor there for many years. And of course, always and only, it was the traditional Latin Mass he celebrated. He re-established contact with SSPX before his death in 2012, when the faithful in his chapels mostly turned to the Society for assistance and service. The irrepressible Father Bolduc, who founded over twenty five chapels in the U.S., who gave generously from his personal assets to provide for mission needs, is remembered here in the U.S. as one of the most stalwart defenders of Catholic tradition against the forces of Modernism.

The story of those gritty early years of SSPX in the U.S. and of Father Bolduc's work can hardly be told without including the priest who teamed with him. Father Carl Pulvermacher was himself an Ember. The veteran priest came to SSPX in 1976 with a love for the Latin Mass that preceded even his entry into the Capuchin order[58] back in 1944. He was ordained a priest in 1952, and assigned in 1965 to a mission at the Crow Indian Reservation in Montana. From that post he served as pastor for six different Indian reservations, his private pilot's license significantly aiding his ability to tend a wide-spread flock. Soon, however, the winds of Vatican II and the New Mass swept over his Indian territories. Father Carl (as he preferred to be called) faced the same issues as all tradition-loving Catholics. For a while, his solution was to say the New Mass publicly and the Old Mass privately. His affinity for the Mass of his ordination was quite clear to his superiors who, out of frustration, transferred him in 1970 back to Saint Anthony's Seminary in Wisconsin. He remained there for two years. During this time, it seems he continued to say private Latin Masses. We may not know exactly how or how often, but we do know that he turned up in Peggy Muehlemann's basement a number of times! Father Carl was one of the stealthy priests occasionally traveling to offer the Latin Mass for desperate Catholics in the very early 1970's.

In late 1972 Father Carl was transferred to Australia where he managed again to serve desperate traditional Catholics with clandestine home Masses.

---

58 Father Carl came from a Wisconsin family of nine children. Three of his brothers also joined the Capuchin Order.

He also happened to make the acquaintance of one Archbishop Marcel Lefebvre when the two were in Sydney in 1974. By late 1975 Father Carl's superiors were exasperated and presented him with an ultimatum: stop saying the Tridentine Mass or leave. He chose to leave. Now independent, Father headed home to Wisconsin where Archbishop Lefebvre and Father Bolduc eventually caught up with him. Father Carl soon joined Father Bolduc at Queen of Angels Church in Dickinson Texas, the base from which they would work together for the next seven years. They would routinely trade off taking seven-to ten-day Mass circuits to mission chapels across the country. Barely two years after his arrival in Dickinson, Father Carl and the team decided that what SSPX needed was a magazine. The first issue of The Angelus was published in 1978 from their spartan Texan office. Father Carl had the lofty title of Managing Editor,[59] which translated to include typesetting, printing, collating, and mailing with assistance from volunteers whenever they could be enlisted.[60] Fortunately for all involved in the enterprise, Father Carl was also a very handy mechanic. A popular feature in The Angelus was Father Carl's own column "Ask Me" answering wide-ranging questions submitted by readers.[61] In 1991 he was asked to move to Davie, Florida and take over the Society's work in that state. Though happy in Texas, the faithful servant accepted. He remained there until his death in 2006 after sixty two years in religious life. This was another tireless human, a quiet and patient man, a Capuchin married to poverty, a priest passionately devoted to the Church and its traditions. Anyone who knew Father Carl Pulvermacher and then read the novel Windswept House, would not be at all surprised to learn that his friend and novelist Malachi Martin had fashioned the fictitious character Father Guttmacher around the indomitable Father Carl Pulvermacher.

---

59   Father Carl fulfilled this role for 12 years until the operation (known later as Angelus Press) was moved to new quarters in Kansas City.

60   Notably, the first 5,000 copies of Michael Davies' Apologia Pro Marcel Lefebvre Volume I were printed and then collated and bound by hand in this shop in a massive undertaking by Father Carl and volunteer parishioners. Picture 256 stacks of paper almost six feet high!

61   An avid reader of this particular column was Archbishop Lefebvre himself!

PART THREE:
FIGHT FOR THE HOMELAND

During all the years that Mary sorted out her own place of worship, she also pursued a separate mission … to see the Latin Mass and other traditions of the Church available once again across the Belleville Diocese. Her heart never stopped aching over what she felt they'd lost. This quest is the other half of Mary's Ember story.

Rewind the calendar to the late 1970's.

CHAPTER 6:
GETTING A FOOTHOLD

STARTING POINT

By the late 1970's, Mary was confident in her convictions about the Catholic faith, so her research efforts were slowing. And she was settled in personally at Queen of the Holy Rosary parish, so demands on that front had subsided. It was realistic to think about addressing a separate issue that had long tormented her … bringing the Latin Mass and other traditions of the Church back to Belleville. The question was, "How?" There wasn't a roadmap for this kind of thing, but she felt certain there were people around who could point her in the right direction. And there were probably people out there who would even pitch in to help - if asked. So she committed to (a) reaching out for advice to any possible source and (b) always paying attention so as to recognize potential allies wherever they might be. With a laser focus on returning the Latin Mass to Belleville, she forged ahead.

What did she have to work with? Not much. She did have her understanding of the Church, its doctrine and practices. But she knew relatively little of how the Catholic Church operated (locally or universally). And she knew very few people who worked in it. In her tool kit at the end of the 1970's, she could really only count one potential ally and some observations she'd made a few years back.

Those observations Mary made years prior related to the Call to Action initiative of the mid-1970's. The Catholic Church, trying its hand at democracy (or the appearance of democracy) undertook a multi-step process to obtain input from all levels of the Church regarding its direction and actions. Steps included regional conferences and parish meetings, all culminating in a major conference in Detroit in 1976. Most would agree it was a calamity, but Mary did identify a few takeaways: the Catholic Church is indeed not a democracy, "delegates" to Church conferences are probably not representative, the Church will stack the deck and influence outcomes despite assurances otherwise, and the liberal wing of the Catholic Church organizes well and speaks loudly. It appeared certain that progressive causes including women's ordination, remarriage by divorced Catholics, and human rights would get the Church's attention going forward.

As for potential allies, Mary had exactly one.[62] Admittedly, even the one was more like a strong hunch. Her name was Mary Ann Winter. The two first met back in 1977, at a dinner speech held at the Shrine of Our Lady of the Snows. They had been invited by a mutual friend,[63] and just happened to sit beside one another at the cloth-covered round eight-top. In chatting, the two managed to discover that they both loved Catholic tradition and the Traditional Latin Mass. In hindsight, both of them would one day point to this evening as a huge milestone in their personal journeys. It was a connection with a soulmate … someone who eventually helped each of them know they weren't alone,[64] that perhaps they weren't crazy, that the situation in the Church might truly be as bizarre as it appeared to them, and that maybe better days were ahead. At that moment in 1977, however,

---

62 That is not to say there was only one other person in Belleville who loved the Latin Mass. In fact, Mary even knew a few Belleville residents who drove to St. Louis (Queen of the Holy Rosary) on Sundays. But they weren't going to invest time and effort on Mary's "project" because, quite frankly, they had given up on the Belleville Diocese and did not trust its leaders. In Mary's words to a friend, "They feel the Bishop is playing games with them and that this implementation of the Indult is intended to satisfy a few cranks until the priests, trained to offer the Latin Mass, die off."

63 The friend was actually a very progressive catholic. He apparently didn't know that Mary and Mary Ann shared a deep affinity for tradition.

64 Their lives were tracking so closely together that both had recently lost hope in Althoff Catholic High School to educate their children in the faith. Mary Ann's daughter had progressed through the school in the class between Mary's fourth and fifth children. Mary had already re-directed her youngest child to public school.

neither of them was on a mission and further collaboration just wasn't top of mind. They parted ways at evening's end, not suspecting their paths would cross again two years later.

On a weekday afternoon in 1979, Mary was strolling through the familiar aisles at Home Brite Hardware Store in search of a few small household items when a vaguely familiar voice called out to her. Turning back toward the broom racks, she quickly recognized Mary Ann Winter. The two did some catching-up, mostly sharing family details they hadn't had time to discuss at the Shrine dinner two years ago. Since their acquaintance originally stemmed from Church matters, Mary thought to ask Mary Ann if she was still interested in the Latin Mass. The reply was quick and clear … she was interested alright, but hadn't heard of any church where this Mass was being allowed. Thinking how true it is that "timing is everything," Mary told her about the new Latin Mass at Queen of the Holy Rosary and invited her to come along any Sunday. The two exchanged phone numbers, not knowing when, or even if, they would be back in touch.

THE OLD PROF AND THE NEW PROSPECT

The rarest commodity in Belleville in the years following Vatican II was a priest expressing any affinity for the Old Mass. Mary knew this all too well, because she had looked for one constantly. Now in the early 1980's her search took on a new meaning. Unless some clergy were on board, appeals to the Bishop for return of the Old Mass, or any elements of Catholic tradition, would probably fall flat. So like an owl on the prowl, Mary looked for any sign of movement in the fields.

Mary first reached out, in late 1979, to a priest from her past. Monsignor Leonard Bauer was pastor of St. Henry's Church on West Main Street in Belleville. But thirty-five years prior he had taught religion at the Academy of Notre Dame to a teenaged Mary. In an ice-breaking letter, Mary acknowledged that, while not currently one of his parishioners, she hoped he might help her based on their common appreciation of the Latin Mass. She noted

"I never once felt that any of our religion teachers doubted the validity or the beauty." She still remembered from those schoolyears "the superlatives used to describe it as the most perfect way to worship and honor God." Mary recounted for him her journey since the mid-1960's including her extensive research, and implored her old teacher to explain why the faithful could not have the Latin Tridentine Mass in Belleville, to point to the party who is supposed to have prohibited it, or to simply show her where she may be in error. She closed humbly and gratefully.

Just days later, a four-page handwritten reply arrived from the monsignor. In it, he provided very extensive, prayerful analysis of the history of the Mass. He made an impassioned case for the essential aspects of the Mass not having been changed, contending that it is still the sacrifice of Calvary. And he expressed true concern for her, counseling her to follow the Pope rather than Archbishop Lefebvre.

Another week later Mary replied in three typed pages, thanking him for his gracious answer and responding politely yet resolutely to all of his central arguments. Her concern, she held, was for her children and grandchildren. And she likened Monsignor Bauer, along with her beloved Monsignor Joseph Orlet, favorably to Archbishop Lefebvre ... all senior prelates not prone to disobedience, but also working incredibly hard for Truth rather than opting for a more comfortable life surely available to them.

Years of silence followed between these two.

About this point in time another priestly prospect popped to Mary's mind. This one stemmed from a letter-to-the-editor in a years-ago edition of The Messenger. The subject of that letter had been Pierre Teilhard de Chardin and the letter writer was Father Emil Maziarz, a priest from Evansville, Illinois, a small village well south of Belleville. In his letter to the editor, Father Maziarz had observed that a previous piece in The Messenger highlighted the teachings of Teilhard de Chardin without cautioning that the French Jesuit priest was an extremely controversial figure, many of his works having been officially banned by Rome as far back as 1939. Father

Maziarz's letter struck a chord with Mary at the time because she had come across Teilhard's name in her studies of Vatican II. So she'd clipped the Maziarz column and into her file it had gone.

In 1980 Teilhard de Chardin was back on Mary's radar, this time due to an announcement from the Diocese of an upcoming lecture series on the author to be given by a Belleville Diocesan scripture scholar. Mary hurriedly read several books by Teilhard and attended the 5 days of lecture, where she was appalled to hear Teilhard unconditionally praised and exalted. Then in 1981 the Messenger reported on a letter by Cardinal Casaroli praising Teilhard, and followed with an article claiming Teilhard had been vindicated. No mention was made of the Monitum that was still in effect.[65] While stewing on all this, Mary remembered the old letter-to-the-editor and went digging. It was still there, a little dusty and hiding among hundreds of old clippings, but she once again had the priest's name. Who knows, she thought, maybe he was an ally-in-waiting?

A letter to Father Maziarz rolled off Mary's Smith Corona in September 1981. Of course, she explained how she'd found his name and shared how Teilhard tied it all together, but stated that her purpose in writing was to ask his advice on how she might help restore the Latin Mass in the diocese. "Like the Monitum on Teilhard," she said, "Quo Primum is surely still in effect."[66]

In his reply a week later, Father Maziarz started by confirming (and firmly documenting) that the Monitum on Teilhard de Chardin was very much still in effect. He then explained that the New Mass (Missal of Paul VI) was the only form allowed to be used, though Latin and Gregorian chant

---

65 1962 *monitum* (warning) by the Holy Office cautioning on Teilhard's works, saying several works of Father Pierre Teilhard de Chardin were being edited and gaining a good deal of success, but abound in such ambiguities and indeed even serious errors, as to offend Catholic doctrine.

66 Quo Primum, Papal Bull of Pope Saint Pius V promulgated in 1570. Referring to the Latin Missal produced from the Council of Trent, key phrases include: "Let all everywhere adopt and observe what has been handed down by the Holy Roman Church…" "We grant and concede in perpetuity that for the chanting or reading of the Mass in any church whatsoever, this Missal is hereafter to be followed absolutely," and its conclusion "Therefore, no one whosoever is permitted to alter this letter, or heedlessly dare go contrary to this notice … Should anyone, however, presume to commit such an act, he should know that he will incur the indignation of Almighty God and of the blessed Apostles Peter and Paul."

were permissible in that liturgy. The Tridentine Mass could only be offered, he said, "with the consent of the Holy Father and he does not give it." He did point to one exception that had come to his attention, "The use of the Missal approved by Pius V is permitted only to priests for reasons of age or for other reasons approved by the ordinary [bishop]. In such permissions, this Missal may be used only at a Mass sine populo [without a congregation]." He went on to defend the Missal of Paul VI and the Pope's right to promulgate it. His typed letter of two full pages was also replete with kind, pastoral guidance including encouragement for Mary "to pray to God for the graces needed to practice obedience to His Vicar on earth, now, John Paul II." With an open invitation to engage in conversation about these matters, he closed, "Let us pray for one another."

Correspondence between these two also went silent for a few years.

GLOBAL GRASSROOTS

After Sunday Mass in the chapel at Queen of the Holy Rosary in the early 1980's, Mary and others would stream down the school hallway toward the steel exit door that opened to the parking lot. During months when school was in session they could view an array of student handiworks taped to the walls. But regardless of the time of year, a four-foot bulletin board midway down the hall was a frequent stopping place for them. Pinned on this board were notices and information from around the world regarding all things Catholic. Information sponge that she was, Mary usually stopped by to peruse the materials. It was here that she first took note of an organization called the Latin Mass Society of England and Wales. The LMS, started in 1965, was one of the real "original McCoys" in the traditional Catholic movement, gathering members in the UK and championing their cause in Rome. Similar groups spawned over time in other countries, usually with similar names. And eventually an umbrella organization[67] surfaced to tie them all together in a loose network. The reach and resources of such organizations were

---

67   FIUV, or Una Voce.

interesting and Mary pondered whether they might help in her mission to bring the Latin Mass back to Belleville. No telling right now, she thought, while banking the information under "potential allies."

In February of 1984, Mary happened across a notice from the Traditional Mass Society, a burgeoning U.S. version of the UK's Latin Mass Society located in San Juan Capistrano, California. The flyer brought news of a new worldwide effort to petition the Vatican for return of the Latin Mass. She quickly wrote an enthusiastic letter to them - offering to do whatever she could to support it. With the letter, she returned her own signed petition, asked for more information,[68] and even enclosed five dollars to defray their expenses. She also apologized, "I'm sorry it can't be more, but I anticipate considerable expense in publicizing this petition drive." Mary's wheels were starting to turn.

Now armed with an official petition, Mary began contacting relatives, friends, neighbors … anyone she knew well who either shared her convictions or was supportive enough to complete and sign the form. The initial pleas having gone well, she thought about reaching beyond her familiar circles for more signatures. Since that effort might draw some attention, she thought it prudent to first request the Bishop's permission to seek signatures "for presentation to him later." She wrote him on February 23rd. The Bishop was ill at the time and she received a reply from the Vicar General of the Diocese, dated March 7th. The reply didn't actually address Mary's request for permission, but did express a strong stand against the Old Mass, ending with, "As you can see, the discipline of the Church has explicitly forbidden the celebration of the so-called 'Latin Tridentine Mass.'" The cleric apparently did not know his audience. He was mistaken, as he likely knew, and as history would one day prove.[69] Mary's reply diplomatically allowed that perhaps she had not stated her request clearly enough, and she proceeded to

---

68 A precise request, identifying materials from the Society's ready-made stockpile such as (#13) sample petitions, (#14) sample letter-to-the-editor campaigns, and (#16) sample letter to send with petition to the newspapers

69 Summorum Pontificum, 2007

succinctly and thoroughly dismantle his position that the Tridentine Mass and its Missal had been sent to the dumpster.[70] The Reverend's three-sentence reply said ... the Bishop's "condition at the present time would not permit him to respond to your request. As Apostolic Administrator of the Diocese, I do not think it is appropriate to authorize such a request and, therefore, I am not giving you permission to collect signatures for such a purpose."

Despite the local resistance, forty-two signed petitions were placed in an envelope, sealed by Mary and mailed to California on April 27th. She stayed on the prowl for more signatures.[71]

Just months later, on October 3, 1984, the international drive for the Latin Mass received an unexpected shot in the arm. In an official letter[72] the Pope bestowed permission on bishops worldwide to allow celebration of the Traditional Latin Mass for the benefit of priests and the faithful. The letter to all bishops explained that the action was intended to be responsive to "the problem of those priests and faithful who had remained attached to the so-called Tridentine Mass" which, despite seeming to be almost completely resolved, nonetheless still continued. Technically, the bishops were being provided an Indult which each bishop could use at his discretion to authorize the Latin Mass. Could this be the breakthrough that traditional Catholics had so long hoped for? Time would tell, but careful readers of the letter cautioned about two particulars; first, the Indult did impose some rather restrictive conditions[73] and second, final authority within any diocese rested with the individual bishop.

70 (MW 2/23/84, 4/2/84) These particular exchanges with the Diocesan Vicar are a shining example of her gentleness, intellect, and communication skills. Over the years, Mary wrote letters and engaged in conversations and debates with a wide array of people, including clergy, publishers, and lay persons.

71 The Traditional Mass Society and Mary kept in touch. She eventually sent over two hundred petitions to them.

72 Known in Latin Mass circles as the Indult of 1984, or Indult 1, the one-page letter was from the Congregation for Divine Worship in Rome to the Presidents of the Catholic Church's Episcopal Conferences. Whether the international petition campaign by Latin Mass Societies played any role in this breaking development was not acknowledged in the letter.

73 The most striking conditions were (a) public evidence must be produced that the priests and faithful have no ties with those who impugn the lawfulness and doctrinal soundness of

So it was now clear the road to the Latin Mass in Belleville ran through the consecrated hands of the Bishop. It seemed a petition drive in the Diocese should be the next step. Mary figured she could help organize a local campaign, and maybe get working right away by canvassing St. Mary's Parish where she knew the terrain. Just then she caught herself. She'd learned some painful lessons in the past 15-plus years and something told her to proceed with caution. She could just imagine being pilloried on a future Sunday from the pulpit at St. Mary's Church as a radical, accused of roaming the streets and alleys of the parish in a subversive effort to undermine the parish and God's holy Church. That vision was a show-stopper for her, considering that her family still attended mass there as did many of her friends. No, she thought, better to follow the chain of command and ensure legitimacy, even at the cost of a slower process. On October 29th, Mary sent a letter introducing herself to St. Mary's new pastor, recapping the Pope's recent Indult and asking when and where the Latin Mass would be available. In a telling response received a month later, he wrote "Please be advised I have spoken to the Diocesan Administrator and the pastors of Belleville. All are agreed that the conditions for having the Latin Mass are not met in our present parish circumstances. The Diocesan Administrator does not foresee any situation in which the use of the Latin Mass would be justified. I suspect the new Bishop will concur with that judgment." Still, Mary kept up correspondence with the pastor. In late March, resolved to initiate some sort of action, she wrote and asked the Pastor directly whether he would give his "permission and authorization to contact the people of St. Mary's with a petition to determine the amount of interest and desire for the Old Mass."[74] Within a week she received his reply, "Please be advised that if you wish to present a petition to the Bishop for a Latin Mass, you do not need my permission. Nor do you need my permission to contact the parishioners.

---

the Roman Missal of 1970, and (b) only the Catholic faithful who are explicitly named in a petition to the Bishop were permitted to attend the Latin Mass.

74   Mary had even asked Russ's approval that she go to the pastor, since Russ and the family probably had more to lose than did she from any ruffled feathers at the Church.

If you wish to pursue this matter, you are free to do it on your own." Case closed, but Mary did feel she was clear to canvas the parish.

The pastor's reply to Mary's request for permission had a very interesting effect, actually marking a milestone in Mary's post-Vatican II journey. When Russ read that reply he decided the Church was in fact being unfair to traditional Catholics. He had felt all along that both the Old and the New Masses ought to be available to those who wanted them. Now he saw the Church as being unreasonable, even heavy-handed, in withholding from its faithful something they had every right to have. Russ had a change of heart. He didn't write letters, or solicit signatures, or engage anyone in public, but he became agreeable and provided moral support for Mary from that day forward.

To the sidewalks Mary went, pastor's letter in one hand, parish directory in the other. Street by street, door by door she marched the territory. Not only was Mary seeking signatures, she was also excited about having a close look at where people stood on the issue. What she found was that about half of the people asked were happy with things as they were, and not interested in signing on. The other half felt the Latin Mass should be available and signed the petition. Her impression was that most of the signers appeared enthusiastic about it. The task turned out to be very time-consuming, but enjoyable.

Now satisfied that a good number of people did want the Old Mass, Mary sent a letter on May 2nd to the bishop and enclosed ninety signed petitions. Having had little success with prior attempts to contact him,[75] and her business now being a bit more official, the package was sent certified mail, return receipt requested, and restricted delivery. This was not a cynical maneuver. Mary just wanted, with all due respect, to ensure the Bishop received this plea from his sheep. On May 7th, Mary received a polite reply, acknowledging receipt and assuring her the letter would "receive the bish-

---

75　For perspective, the Bishop was new, having only been in office since December. Perhaps he had not seen either of Mary's two prior letters welcoming him and asking about the potential for the Latin Mass in Belleville. In any case, she had not received a response to either letter.

op's careful attention at his earliest convenience." She could hardly see this as encouraging, but remained undeterred (writing at the time to a friend "patience and persistence is my motto – I think I've retained my sense of humor through all this, although it might be more correctly termed madness.") The following week she sent another letter to the Bishop, this one with ten more petitions.[76]

Just a week after the second letter the phone rang at Mary's house, the caller identifying himself as the Bishop's priest-secretary. He informed her that the Bishop was "working on setting up details of the Mass and that Mary would receive this information as soon as it is available." He also mentioned that it would not be necessary to send in any more petitions. A letter arrived for Mary the very next day, May 22, 1985.

TLM ON MAIN STREET

Below the Bishop's letterhead was the following:

… I hereby authorize the Tridentine Mass to be celebrated on the first Saturday of June, July, and August of 1985 in St. Henry Church, 5315 West Main Street Belleville. The time will be 9:00 a.m. each of the three months. I hereby designate Reverend Monsignor Leonard A. Bauer to be the celebrant of the Mass on these occasions.

In accordance with the instructions of the Sacred Congregation of Worship, there is to be no public advertisement of the Mass beyond the group which has petitioned for the Mass.

Monsignor Bauer suggests that you provide two Mass servers who are familiar with the proper response. Further, any singing during the Mass must be in Latin.

---

76 She sent it certified mail, return receipt requested but dropped the restricted delivery this time.

I ask almighty God to bless you and your family and in this month of May may Our Lady lovingly watch over you and your loved ones. With warmest good wishes and kind regards …

The stalemate was broken. Not a huge commitment, but certainly something. In any case, there was no time to reflect … the first Mass was one week away! Mary was both elated and panicked. She needed to get word out and find servers and arrange for music and probably a few other tasks she couldn't envision at the moment and – oh – it was dinner time. First she told Russ, who was surprised and happy for her - and thoughtfully offered to make his own dinner that night. Then she got busy. She started by calling several men from St. Mary's parish who had served the Latin Mass back in the day. To her chagrin, each of them declined to have anything to do with it. Feeling the need for a little positive headway, she decided to recruit an ally. "Hello, Mary Ann? This is Mary. You won't believe what showed up in the mail today …" Mary Ann joined in the elation and in the panic. Then she made a huge contribution. Without batting an eye, she volunteered her husband Smitty to serve the Mass.[77] Mary and Mary Ann went on to strategize how to inform people who might be interested. Mary Ann offered to contact people she knew in Mascoutah and some old friends in St. Teresa parish. Mary would work from her lists of petition-signers from the past year, suggesting she would have about one hundred phone calls to make. A busy week lay ahead for both of them.

Mary began her phone calls the next day, and squeezed in a mid-morning call to Monsignor Bauer to coordinate with him. It had been almost five years since they'd written each other with thoughts about the Latin Mass. Mary didn't know what to expect or even how Monsignor Bauer had come to be selected for this role.[78] He greeted her warmly and immediately the

---

77 Smitty had learned to serve the Latin Mass *many* years prior at St. Teresa Church in Belleville. No one ever heard exactly whether there was any trepidation on his part about fulfilling his wife's promise. He, in turn, recruited his cousin to assist.

78 Mary never did uncover what machinations led to Msgr. Bauer's assignment to this Mass. She would come to find later, however, that Msgr. Bauer and some other area priests had kept their Latin Rite skills sharp over time.

two began to plan for the upcoming Mass. Monsignor Bauer assured Mary he would handle all logistics on the altar, and he was delighted to hear about his veteran adult server. He, in turn, delighted Mary by volunteering to arrange for the music himself. Mary also called her old friends at the Traditional Mass Society in California who offered a bit of welcome moral support and said they would provide additional lists, by zip code, of any interested persons in their files.

On June 1, 1985, for the first time in over fifteen years, a public Traditional Latin Mass was held in Belleville. It was a Low Mass following the 1962 Missal in a Church where most of the traditional architecture remained. As former pastor at St. Henry's, Monsignor Bauer may have been the reason that the altar, tabernacle and communion rails were still intact. It was a glorious occasion for a local Ember and all the 75 or so people who attended.[79] Background music played (appropriate to the Low Mass) and the organist sang Panis Angelicus at the Offertory. Monsignor Bauer offered the Mass with the reverence and beauty everyone had been hoping to experience.[80] Smitty and his cousin were near-flawless in serving. After Mass, Mary waited for the organist to descend from the balcony in order to meet and thank her. The two chatted for several minutes. Mrs. Timmer was, it turns out, thrilled to be asked to play at their Mass. Furthermore, she wanted to be clear she was providing her services for free, and she could play every first Saturday ... it happened to fulfill a long-standing commitment of hers.[81] It was a memorable day.

Looking ahead to the second monthly Mass, there was one significant request for change. Monsignor Bauer wanted future Masses to be High

---

79 Headcount by the organist.

80 Msgr. Bauer spoke before Mass, telling all those present "If anyone present does not recognize the Pope as the Head of the Church, or does not recognize the New Mass as a valid Mass, this Mass is not for you and you shouldn't be here." Two people walked out.

81 The organist later shared a private matter with Mary. Earlier in life, the Blessed Virgin Mother had answered a very important prayer. In thanks, she had promised to play the organ at Mass every first Saturday for the rest of her life. Since the Diocese had virtually dropped all Saturday Masses (after instituting the Saturday Vigil Mass), she had struggled to find opportunities to fulfill her commitment.

Masses. He loved the sacred music of the High Mass. Key to accomplishing this was the organist and yet again the team struck gold. The organist was amply qualified, she was happy to inform them.[82] She would sing it herself and provide music sheets to all attendees for them to join in as much as possible.

Three months passed and three beautiful Latin Masses were held at St. Henry's. Attendance dropped by about one half for the second Mass and stabilized there, a phenomenon that Mary attributed mostly to the Masses being on Saturday. She colorfully described attendance in a letter to Monsignor Bauer as "an indication that nothing short of a nuclear war will motivate the average Catholic to attend Mass, other than their Sunday obligation." For some who did attend the monthly Mass, however, new and lasting bonds were forged. The first Mass in June was the occasion when Russ met Smitty. They became fast friends as their wives had, and the two couples enjoyed years of faith, fun, and travel together. They also anchored an after-Mass lunch every first Saturday, open to anyone and regularly drawing 10-12 people.

Just before the third Mass, in August of 1985, Monsignor Bauer made a brief but important announcement. "The first-Saturday Mass here at St. Henry's will continue indefinitely." This answered a lingering question for these faithful, since the original approval had run its course. They were relieved and happy. From Mary's viewpoint, the announcement was interesting in that it not only answered a question, but raised another. For the past three months, she and her friends had refrained from asking the Bishop directly whether the Mass would continue past August. They simply didn't want to stir the pot. Since, no doubt, the Bishop had now approved, someone must have consulted with him and perhaps even encouraged him. Once again, the backstage machinations would never really be explained, but most of those faithful in the pews believe that Monsignor Bauer went to bat

---

82 Not only did she know the music for the Latin High Mass, but she would also prove to be a gifted singer.

for the cause.[83] Those who knew him, the man whose career started over 40 years earlier preaching evenings in the streets across rural southern Illinois, would not have been surprised.

---

83 They also suspected Msgr. Bauer may have had a hand in The Messenger posting advance notice of the Mass each month, a pleasant surprise to the organizers.

CHAPTER 7:
HARD SLOG TO PRESENT DAY

WHO AMONG YOU?

In her research and activities during the 1980's, Mary occasionally came across something written by a Belleville Diocesan priest (or information *about* one of the priests) that hinted he might lean toward Tradition, or at least have a healthy respect for it. She looked at any such find as a prospective teacher for her. And maybe, she thought, even a potential ally in the quest to restore the Latin Mass in their mutual backyard. In addition to Monsignor Bauer, four other Belleville priests played interesting roles as Mary navigated the 1980's in Belleville.

BISHOP JOHN WURM

John N. Wurm, Auxiliary Bishop of St. Louis was named the new Bishop of Belleville in 1981. For Mary, who was still just getting started with the push to restore the Latin Mass to Belleville, it seemed like an opportunity to get a feel for where the new Bishop might stand on the issue. Besides, their paths had crossed twice in just the past nine months (a wedding Mass he had offered and a family tour of his Cathedral in St. Louis), so she had two excellent ice-breakers that would even serve as examples for points she wanted to make. She quickly crafted a letter with her examples, openly signaling her traditional leanings, and then described the circumstances in Belleville as she saw them at the time. Candid always, she told the incoming Bishop, "I feel you have been handed a tough assignment, Modernism in the Church in Belleville has been running rampant." Offering prayer and support, she closed with the hope that those in Belleville who wished to attend the Mass of their youth might again be able to do so. Within a week she received a reply, acknowledging their past intersections and the points she made. He didn't provide much hope about the Latin Mass being offered, assuring her only of "fidelity to the Holy Father and to the Magisterium of the Church." Better than bad, thought Mary, but not actually good.

The new Bishop moved from St. Louis to Belleville and assumed duties in the Fall. Mary decided to write him again late in October. This time she didn't even want a reply, she said, asking only "that you will arrange an avenue of communication with the people who are unhappy with, or have questions about, the changes in the Church." And then she filled two pages with family travails in the new Church that in part explained her passions. She followed in January with another letter, this time sticking to facts and arguments about the Mass and Vatican II. And this time she received a cordial hand-written note from the Bishop, thanking her for her input and describing the Latin Mass matter as beyond his capacity, "Only the Pope can do something about it." Maybe better than bad, but definitely not good, thought Mary.

Then in Mid-February an unexpected envelope showed up in Mary's mailbox. Inside, were papers with a sticky note bearing the letterhead "from the Desk of ... Most Reverend John N. Wurm". The handwriting said, "Dear Mary, I just received this and thought you might like to read it." Enclosed was a copy of the Latin Mass Survey Report[84] issued in January by the U.S. Bishop's Committee on the Liturgy in Washington D.C. Mary proceeded to analyze the document, leading her to sixteen key observations. In her reply to the Bishop, she thanked him immensely for his generosity and for his

---

84   The international survey, conducted by the Vatican in the summer and fall of 1980 to gather information about the Latin Rite Mass (such as use, interest, etc.) asked for responses from every Bishop. Responses from 1,750 bishops were included in the report. The Bishop of Belleville at the time did not publicize the existence of the survey nor was input requested from the faithful in the diocese. The Messenger carried a tiny notice about the worldwide survey in its October 31, 1980, edition.

interest and concern in her dilemma. She provided him a copy of her page of notes. And in three typewritten pages, she expounded on the notes while adding, for his information, detail of some new real-life experiences from the Church in Belleville. The Bishop sent Mary a brief note in response, acknowledging receipt and telling her he did read it with interest. Hoping the Bishop was "still willing to listen to the least of your flock," Mary sent another letter in July. Her topic was the discouraging experiences she'd had in the first several sessions of the Diocese's new Catechist Certification Program. Three pages of detail followed. A week later, Mary received a beefy two-page response from the Bishop, carefully addressing each of her concerns. He agreed with some of her points to an extent, but generally defended the program as "a reasonable imparting of the message of the Church". Though a bit discouraging in its conclusion, the thoughtfulness of their exchanges still provided encouragement for Mary. Whether real progress lay ahead was an open question.

The correspondence continued. Mary posted a letter in September, starting with thanks and humble acceptance of having been wrong on the points she'd made in her prior letter. This time, she just asked that the Bishop allow her to make a few final points and she promised to "never bother you again." She conveyed the story of her family, their church, and their schools in the years since Vatican II, and closed with two requests. First, that he meet with a priest of the Society of St. Pius X ("as the Latin Mass Report indicated the Bishops are willing to do.") Second, that he provide suitable facilities for a priest of the Society to offer Mass in Belleville. Two weeks later Mary received a note from Bishop Wurm politely informing her that he had received her letter, but had been in and out of town so much and tending to business in the Diocese that he hadn't had time to look up and research the questions she raised in the letter. She could "be assured that you will receive an answer from me."

That was the last official correspondence Mary received from Bishop Wurm. In 1983 he became ill, and he died of cancer in April of 1984. Mary was left to imagine what kind of impact this generous and righteous man might have had on the Diocese of Belleville.

MONSIGNOR HARRY JEROME

Mary first heard of Monsignor Harry Jerome[85] when he arrived at St. Mary's as the new pastor in 1984. Her early correspondence with him, from October 1984 through March 1985, involving permission to petition door-to-door in the parish, was described previously. It had been a rocky start, and Monsignor Jerome wasn't presently in her "potential allies" file.

But if anything, Mary was persistent. Just weeks after their exchanges regarding petitions, Monsignor Jerome included in the weekly bulletin a list of five "takeaways" from a pastor's workshop recently held in Chicago, along with an invitation to St. Mary parishioners to comment on them as they felt related to their parish. Mary couldn't resist. She crafted a reply that presented five points, each in direct contradiction to the workshop's points. And then she observed that her list was clearly pre-Vatican II and the pastors' list clearly post-Vatican II. It was also inarguable that her list described a parish that was pastor-led, vocation-rich, and sacrament-focused. The opposite was clearly true of the pastors' workshop list. To this Mary attached one of her fondest scripture phrases … "by their fruits we shall know them." In three single-spaced typed pages that followed, Mary recounted the methodical dismantling of the Catholic Mass wrought "in the spirit of Vatican II," citing chilling parallels to strategy employed in the Protestant Reformation.[86] She recalled for her pastor that the Tridentine Mass had never been prohibited by the Pope. No reply came from the pastor. Disappointing but not necessarily surprising, she thought. Besides, about this time Mary was knee-deep

---

85 Msgr. Jerome was ordained in 1961, received post-graduate schooling in Canon Law at the Catholic University in Washington, D.C., had worked in two diocesan parishes, and prior to this assignment completed a 10-year stint in the Diocesan Marriage Tribunal.

86 Cranmer by Hilaire Belloc, 1931, Lippincott (p.234). " We must remember that the object kept steadily before their eyes was the abolition of the Mass; but the Mass … could not be got rid of at a blow … it was necessary to insinuate, to go step by step, to substitute the totally new thing for the old thing by degrees." On page 235 "Next, one little point after another would have to be introduced to gradually break-up the Mass as men had known it."

in petition drives with the Traditional Latin Mass Society and so wasn't concerning herself much with the goings-on at St. Mary's. She did keep an eye, however, on the weekly bulletin carried home by Russ every Sunday.

The bulletin from St. Mary's carried news one day later in the year, August of 1985 when it was announced that Monsignor Jerome would be taking a leave of absence to receive treatment for an alcohol addiction. An eerie several months ensued at St. Mary's, waiting to see if or when their pastor would return while his assistant minded the store. During the pastor's time away, the bulletin occasionally included an update from Monsignor Jerome, always expressing his gratitude for prayers and letters received from his friends at St. Mary's. Monsignor Jerome returned at the end of January 1986, in good condition and good spirits, ready to resume his work. All seemed to be back on track for Monsignor Jerome and for St. Mary's. April saw the departure of the assistant Pastor to begin post-graduate studies.[87]

Over the ensuing months Mary sensed something curious in those weekly bulletins. In June came a direct appeal from Monsignor Jerome to parishioners to attend Thursday Night Novena to Our Mother of Perpetual Help. The Novena was a long and proud tradition at St. Mary's, but participation had waned in recent years. The Pastor's appeal was repeated the following week, along with encouragement to pray the rosary together with family every day. And then again, on a third consecutive Sunday, the Novena appeal got louder, this time with a full history of why it was started by Monsignor Joseph Orlet fifty-one years earlier.[88] The pastor urged his flock to "humble ourselves, kneel before her Shrine, and beg her help" as they

---

87 Two years later, the ex-assistant pastor wrote to the parishioners to inform them he would not be returning to the Diocese. He planned to leave the priesthood and start a career in social work. In the letter he petitioned, "I also ask your forgiveness for breaking my promise to you to serve as a priest until death." Mary wondered whether anyone noticed to whom he said he had made a promise.

88 Young Joseph Orlet, ordained at the age of 22, was rushed through the seminary because there was such a need for priests in the diocese at the time. Having been overworked in the seminary, he became very ill early in his priesthood. For six months he walked to Church, but was too weak to offer Mass. In his prayers he told the Blessed Virgin that if he were to recover and be able to resume his duties, he would start a novena in her honor in whatever parish he was assigned.

attend the 6:30p.m. Novena and the Holy Mass that followed. In October, shortly before Pope John Paul II's Assisi conference, the Pastor's message rallied parishioners to support the peace initiative by concrete actions on that day - praying for peace, coming to Mass, praying the rosary, offering acts of penance and self-sacrifice for peace. "We must believe that God is ready to hear our prayers which we offer without ceasing." There was a new and strange gravity about it all.

It was late 1986 now. The St. Henry's first-Saturday Mass was well-established, but wasn't likely to be approved by the Bishop for Sundays, so time had come for Mary to seek new avenues for the Latin Mass in Belleville. She wasn't sure what, if anything, to make of the situation at St. Mary's or with Monsignor Jerome in particular, but it had been awhile since she last corresponded with him and she still hoped to make some progress at her home parish. Mary wrote to her Pastor with an update and a plea. The update covered progress made so far with the Bishop. The plea was for action by Monsignor Jerome. She explained shortcomings of the current situation, specifically the continued absence of a Sunday Latin Mass anywhere in the Diocese. Then she reminded him of the great number of signed petitions she'd collected. "Please," she implored, "beseech the Bishop on our behalf." Two days later came a surprise request from Monsignor Jerome ... for a copy of the Pope's Indult. He seemed curious. She was encouraged, and promptly sent him a copy of the Indult. For good measure, she also enclosed copies of St. Pius V's Quo Primum and Pope Paul VI's Missale Romanum since, to her thinking, these two documents were central to the "confusion in the Church today." The holidays passed without any response.

Just as January broke, a letter arrived for Mary. Monsignor Jerome had been busy, and he had indeed beseeched the Bishop. He expressed regret that the reply he received from the diocese was not positive, and wondered aloud whether the Bishops had really listened to people like Mary and tried to understand the depth of feeling they had.[89] He also expressed distaste

---

89   Msgr. Jerome also enclosed a copy of a "Framework" the Province of Illinois had issued to govern requests for the Tridentine Mass, dated 2/26/85, and provided to Msgr. Jerome

for the tone of the reply, which included the statement "I hope this will resolve the matter at hand once and for all." Monsignor Jerome, while clearly unhappy with what he'd heard, was oddly enthusiastic. He volunteered to Mary that he did plan to write the Bishop again, if only to ask the Bishop to listen to those who are pleading. And he said he'd be listening carefully at the upcoming Laity Synod where he understood "this topic is going to be raised by some of the laity."[90] He ended with every good wish and an invitation to call him if she wished to discuss the matter further. If ever a rejection came with a silver lining, Monsignor Jerome encouraging Mary in her efforts was a welcome one.

Two developments had emerged by January of 1987, and they would continue unabated through the year. First, Monsignor Harry Jerome was pressing St. Mary's parish in a more traditional direction. The second is directly correlated to the first. Mary and Russ and others who had come to love and respect Monsignor Jerome grew more concerned about his welfare. It was clear that Monsignor Jerome's sermons were becoming more "conservative" or "traditional," and even his bulletin writings carried bolder messages. In May the pastor used almost a full column in the bulletin to espouse the virtues of Brown Scapular devotion. In August a column on Marian devotion coupled with more nudging for families to attend the Thursday Novena. Other "new" messages to his flock included orthodox perspectives on the Mass and direction to all to say the morning offering prayer each day. Throughout the year, Monsignor Jerome sought to inject more reverence into the Mass. For all this, the pastor received enormous criticism from the parishioners.

Russ and Mary heard about it, and Mary understood it perfectly from her earlier days. Beginning in February, Mary wrote letters to Monsignor Jerome supporting him but begging him not to "have any trouble on my

---

with the diocese's reply. The framework lays down eight additional constraints over and above those in the Pope's Indult. While several may have seemed extreme, item D was the whopper ... "The Mass may not take place on Sunday or Holy Days of Obligation."

90 Reference 1987 Synod for the Laity later in this chapter to see how the Synod played out.

account." She asked him not to press the issue of the Latin Mass with the Bishop, stating she would continue that struggle. She would do what she could regarding the Latin Mass, she said, "but I am certainly resigned to God's Will once I have done all I am capable of doing." She shared her belief God will never forsake His Church. In other letters through the year, she and Russ expressed concern and offered any help they could provide.

In January of 1988, Monsignor Harry Jerome was suddenly removed as pastor at St. Mary's… though he surfaces again later in an equally important role in our story!

FATHER STU

In February 1985 Mary first reached out to a priest who turned out to be an enigma, so much so that it may be best to refer to him simply as Father Stu. Mary had recently read an interesting article newly penned by the well-educated Father Stu. He had actually studied the documents of Vatican II, so they had common ground to be sure. Assuming he would not have time for individual meetings, she asked in a letter if he would please let her know should he ever conduct a seminar or lecture course. Father Stu's quick and gracious handwritten response was a bit of a surprise, especially when he admitted that he, too, had issues with the way in which Vatican II had been implemented. Mary attended a lecture series by Father Stu that spring, and the two began corresponding regularly. Very early in their communications Mary urged Father Stu to conduct a lecture series on the Sacred Mass and Vatican II, saying, "Since you are the most orthodox priest I have encountered in this diocese, I am anxious to attend your lecture and hopefully find where I am in error." Their banter carried on through 1985 - Mary pressing him about the New Mass disaster, Father Stu agreeing with her that problems exist, and reiterating that they lay in the implementation of the Vatican II documents. Near year's end, and just before he left for Rome, Father Stu suggested Mary read "The Ratzinger Report" and the two could discuss it after Christmas.

1986 and 1987 brought more exchanges between the two, but maybe just as important were actions by Father Stu that proved his orthodox grounding. In one such action, he took a public stance on a doctrinal issue raised in a book review in the Messenger. Not only did he refute the book, he refuted the reviewer – who happened to be a diocesan colleague. Father Stu was firmly on the orthodox side of this dust-up. Mary continued to gain confidence in this priest who wrote to her the following in gratitude for support shown to him:

> *"I thank God for the others – laymen and women especially – who have defended this Pontiff and this little priest ... really defending the Incarnation of The Word Himself. We need many, many more." ... "My deepest concern is for the young, who are exposed to "catechisms" and catechists who do not present the whole Truth."*

Along the way Father Stu took another notable public stance in a lengthy and brilliant publication on multiple subjects including: the meaning of the Mass (first and foremost a sacrifice at an Altar), proper reverence for the Mass (as the mystery of the ages, not to be trivialized or adapted to modern mentality), a Priest's core identity ("sacrificer"), and especially the purpose behind the role of altar boy (a young man who, kneeling beside the priest, hears the call to become a priest). It stood out as forthright teaching - in a diocese that nonetheless leaped to insert altar girls a few years later.

A highlight among their exchanges was a five page manifesto from Mary to Father Stu in mid-1987 wherein she summarized many of her most troubling concerns and strongest arguments while simultaneously posing questions about The Ratzinger Report and implicating The Messenger. Father Stu replied two days later with a hardy thank you, reserving time to re-read and study it. And on they went with exchanges that managed to stay truly warm and respectful despite testing each other on hefty subject matter ranging from the difference between "real effects" and "sensible consolations", to whether a council can be separated from its "spirit," to communion-in-the-hand, to the best texts for educating the young. They readily shared reading suggestions and conference recommendations. And always they offered prayers for each other, because they were each tackling troublesome challenges.

In personal correspondence with Mary, Father Stu had proven himself to be a caring and tradition-minded priest. He'd been consistently passionate about the whole Truth of the Catholic faith, which did include a respect for tradition. But, as we said earlier, he eventually turned out to be something of an enigma. This is because of his public actions after the year 2000 - actions that appeared to be wholly in "the spirit of Vatican II." In the years that followed, there were no longer signs of a love of tradition, private or public, from Father Stu (at least from Mary's vantage point). Nevertheless, when Mary thought of Father Stu after that, she always returned to a sentiment she had written to him back in March 1990, "You have been a beacon of light in these dark times." He had certainly been for her, for a period of time. Mary hoped that somehow Father Stu continued to shine, even if it were in places she couldn't see.

FATHER EMIL MAZIARZ

The southeast corner of Belleville's main square is dominated by a six-story art deco-styled building. A civic landmark, the Hotel Belleville opened in 1931 as a modern hotel to draw businessmen and conventions to town. Having served its purpose for over thirty years, the building was sold to the Diocese of Belleville in 1961. The diocese converted the hotel into a modern retirement facility and named it The Meredith Home. The popular home usually maintained a waiting list for tenants, so getting Russ' mother into the Meredith Home in 1984 was a comfort for everyone. It also brought about an unexpected reunion. During a visit to her mother-in-law, Mary discovered that the chaplain at the Meredith Home was one Father Emil Maziarz. Mary's remarkable memory had no trouble recalling that name from their brief correspondence some three years prior. She usually viewed these types of occurrences as God bringing people together on His schedule, so she left a note at the desk for the chaplain, saying hello and inviting him to call her at his convenience. Later in the week, Father Maziarz called. The two had a nice chat, and left it that Mary would arrange a visit for them in the next week or two.

Scheduling that meeting with Father Maziarz in mid-summer proved a little more difficult than anticipated, so Mary took to her typewriter to get thoughts rolling. Five single-spaced pages later, she had poured out her concerns and positions on many issues of the day, including responses to some of his comments from three years prior. Father replied quickly with a note telling her that he would be on vacation until mid-August, and hoping they could meet then to discuss the contents of her letter. And they did. Sitting in a study off the main lobby at the Meredith Home, the two new acquaintances poured over topics from politics to theology. What they found was agreement on virtually everything. Except - wouldn't you know - the New Mass. Father Maziarz expounded on rationales ranging from obedience to natural turmoil following councils. Mary countered with obeying God rather than man, and relative peace following Trent. And so these two continued. Deciding that they were not going to agree on the New Mass, the chaplain rose and walked to his book shelves. His hand went straight for his classically-bound copy of The Holy Sacrifice of the Mass by Rev. Dr. Nicholas Gihr, copyright 1902. As long as she took good care if it and returned it, he said, she should read this book. She thanked him and promised to comply, excepting for the fact that it might take a while because she tends to take many notes as she reads. They parted with promise of a future meeting.

Meet again they did, early in December after the two had exchanged letters and each done a bit of homework. They still agreed on everything except the New Mass. On that subject Mary had a question for the kind priest, after having read the Gihr book. It seemed to her that the book merely confirmed everything she believed about the Mass. When she said this, he replied "I am under a vow of obedience to the Bishop." He would say no more. She could draw her own conclusions. She did, and she was galvanized in her direction. The two parted again, this time without plans to meet again. They did correspond a bit later, but Father Maziarz would continue to formally advise Mary that the Novus Ordo Mass was valid and that she should not follow Archbishop Marcel Lefebvre.

Not long after Mary had gotten guidance from Father Maziarz at the Meredith Home, she and a couple friends recruited the knowledgeable priest to teach catechesis to them. He generously agreed and met with them many times in his study at the Meredith Home. They treasured his sound, orthodox teaching on the catechism, and their study went cover-to-cover. Father Maziarz retired from active duty in the early 1990's and took up residence at the Hincke-Sense Home, a diocesan center for retired Priests. While he was there, he had one last exchange with Mary. Mary called him in November of 1992 because she'd heard that Father Maziarz was saying the Traditional Latin Mass privately each day at the Hincke Home. After a little catching up, Mary explained the main reason for her call. She'd heard he offers the Latin Mass, and might she be able to attend one of them? Nothing Mary had been through in the past several decades had prepared her for his response. First silence. Then a deep breath. Then, nearly sobbing, the gentle priest made a heart-wrenching plea, "Please, Mary, DO NOT come. I fear I would lose my privilege." The permission to say his beloved Latin Mass privately was likely the most important thing in this retired priest's life. As much as Mary wanted nothing more than to find a daily Latin Mass, the subject changed immediately. Father Maziarz died in 1996. He'd been a blessing, in his own way, for Mary and others through some tough years. It struck Mary as a little bit of justice and mercy reaching down to earth when Monsignor Bauer beautifully offered Father Maziarz' funeral Mass ... a Latin Requiem High Mass.

RIP CURRENT

The everyday life of an Ember in Belleville could be compared to a swimmer in the ocean ... who suddenly realizes the water is too deep, *and* the shore is too far away, *and* he is stuck in a rip current. A rip current is a strong and localized zone of water moving directly *out* to sea, thus countering efforts to get to shore. It can be frustrating and even dangerous if not recognized. The most effective way to conquer one is to move out of the zone by swimming parallel to the shore. A person caught in one could even lose hope.

Since Vatican II, the Belleville Diocese has been a rip current zone for any Ember. Every effort to respect or promote Catholic tradition has faced a head-on force ... the Diocese's zealous devotion to "the spirit of Vatican II." It would be hard to fully appreciate Mary's fight for the homeland without pondering what it was like to swim in its rip current.

ECUMENISM – FIRST, ALWAYS

Vatican II inspired an array of movements. One of them, ripe for Belleville's zeal, was ecumenism.[91] While the Vatican was experiencing fits-and-starts at the global level, some national Bishops' conferences were encouraging action at the diocesan level. Belleville entered the game early when its Bishop held a "Red Mass" ecumenical service for judges and lawyers, held at St. Peter's Cathedral in 1977. Following that first act, The Messenger periodically announced other ecumenical events being added to the Bishop's schedule. Especially notable was his participation in multiple events for "Reformation Sunday" in 1980, the 450th Anniversary of the Augsburg Confession.[92] At the first event he spoke to a local Lutheran Congregation in their church. Interviewed in The Messenger about it, he reflected, "The Augsberg Confession has particular significance for Lutheran/Roman Catholic relations since the hope of those who wrote and endorsed it was that the Lutheran Reform movement would be seen and develop as a movement within the one Catholic Church."[93] He continued, "The Catholic Church has taken some big steps that were called for during Luther's time in the Liturgy

---

91 Efforts seeking to unify the Catholic Church with other Christian faiths, improve cooperation with non-Christian faiths.

92 The Augsberg Confession is the primary confession of faith of the Lutheran Church and one of the most important documents of the Protestant Reformation, first published in the year 1530.

93 The document was not accepted as such by the Roman Catholic authorities of that day.

and the Eucharist." Those words may have been inspirational to some faithful Catholics, but to the ears of an Ember the Bishop was signaling camaraderie at an unthinkable cost. Later, the Bishop participated in another, even bigger, celebration of the same 450th milestone for Lutherans. He joined with St. Louis Archbishop May and Lutheran Presidents and Bishops for a major Ecumenical Celebration at the historic Old Cathedral in St. Louis. A Catholic monsignor said to the assembly, "We are here not to celebrate 450 years of division but to celebrate our growing closer." The service was followed by a fine reception at the Marriott Pavilion Hotel on South Broadway.

Of course, ecumenical activity was occurring at higher levels of the Catholic Church and these would also be trumpeted in Belleville whenever possible. Things like the 1983 U.S. Catholic – Lutheran Consensus on Justification, and the 1986 Assisi Conference organized by the Pope. A local Ember like Mary would process such information, most often simply dismayed at the progressive happenings she surely could not influence, then wait anxiously to see how soon and in what manner the Belleville Diocese would take related action.

Ecumenism gained even more momentum in Belleville in the mid-80's. A steady stream of advocacy for ecumenism and special ecumenical events pervaded the Diocese. A representative sampling of ecumenism on the march in southern Illinois:

- Even before the Vatican began pressing to expand Lutheran-Catholic dialogue[94] at the local parish level in the early 1980's, the Belleville Diocese had already formed its local/regional steering committee.

- The Bishop continued visiting and speaking at Protestant houses of worship including Presbyterian, United Church of Christ, and Lutheran.[95]

---

94 Note: Lutheran/Catholic dialogue had been happening at the highest levels since Vatican II. "Progress" had been well-documented in the Catholic news periodicals.

95 It was also apparently newsworthy that "special vocal music" was provided by the Bishop's assistant, Msgr. Schwaegel, at two United Church of Christ services.

- The Metro-East *Catholic* Prayer Groups, in planning for their annual Fall Day of Prayer in Trenton, courteously served notice in the newspaper of a change to their routine, "Since this year's Day of Prayer will be an ecumenical outreach, there will not be a Mass celebrated."

- A meeting between St. Luke's Catholic and St. Mark's Lutheran parishioners, followed by a joint prayer service and a procession from one church to the other carrying a banner marking the signing of the joint declaration on the Doctrine of Justification.

- Catholic, Episcopalian, and Lutheran pastors teamed in a Good Friday "Ecumenical Statement" to carry a cross together several blocks to St. Luke's Church.

- A "Centennial Ecumenical Celebration" was held at St. Peter's Cathedral in 1987, a major event (including five Protestant denominations and 1,300 total participants) hosted by the Bishop. The occasion marked the 100 year anniversary of the *Catholic Diocese* in Belleville. Hailed by attendees as a "journey toward unity" and a "real resurgence of ecumenical spirit coming from the Catholic Church".

- Lutheran services held in a Catholic gymnasium. Holy Childhood parish generously lent its gym/auditorium and cafeteria to newly-formed St. Martin of Tours Lutheran Parish, a congregation without a church after splitting with the conservative arm of their own Lutheran Church. The Catholics and Lutherans shared coffee and donuts after Mass on the first Sunday of Advent.

- Articles in The Messenger, mouthpiece of the Bishop, advocated for unification, providing expert insights such as "Catholics have been elected President of prestigious Protestant bible societies such as the Society of Biblical Literature and Protestants like Paul Achtemeier, have headed up the Catholic Biblical Association."[96] Progress to some perhaps, but the Ember sensed compromise and water-down.

---

96 1991 The Messenger.

An Ember living in Belleville, awash in this ecumenism, mostly thought "why?"

Mary saw Ecumenism as a slippery and dangerous thing. There was a good type and a bad type. It could be good and perfectly in keeping with Catholic beliefs, if unification was to be achieved by conversion of others to Catholicism. St. Paul would approve wholeheartedly. On the other hand, ecumenism would be bad if – in the quest for unification – Catholics were to compromise their core beliefs in the name of unity. Embers hold that if the Catholic Faith is changed, it ceases to be actually Catholic. It wouldn't make sense anymore, if even changed by small degrees. Unfortunately, the approach by the global Catholic Church's highest authorities showed no indication of the good type of ecumenism. In fact their actions were already signaling the bad type. And for all appearances, the Belleville Diocese was happily following suit. It was a constant drumbeat that tortured the ears of an Ember.

BEYOND ECUMENISM

The ecumenism movement was a very big deal in Mary's view, and it was constant, and it was exasperating.

Even so, it was still just ONE of MANY underlying forces in the rip current she faced every day.

- There was also ... **Modernist teaching**

    ... continuous and unapologetic, in schools and adult workshops,[97] by usually haughty and frequently forceful Diocesan scholars. One high-level priest, commenting on Humanae Vitae, told his class "I don't think a bunch of celibate men should be telling married people what to do," and suggested the class determine such things for themselves. When challenged that a celibate man had

---

97 All references are taken from Mary's contemporaneous notes and transcribed audio recordings of classes. Unusually dedicated documentation to be sure, but Mary simply couldn't believe what she was hearing. Commentaries by these priests in publications, including The Messenger, over the years typically conveyed similar beliefs and attitudes.

founded the Church, the cleric asked, "Do we really know Christ was celibate?" amusing both the priest and his class. Another high-ranking Diocesan priest,[98] an advocate of progressive thinkers such as Hans Kung and Pierre Teilhard de Chardin, teaching a class about the books of the Gospel said, "Each evangelist wrote because he didn't agree with the prior evangelist. I guarantee you that the evangelists never thought they were on an equal basis." Expounding on that with the example of John's Gospel regarding the return of Jesus, he went on:

> "You don't have to believe what John teaches on this. You can believe what Matthew teaches, or Paul. Now my personal belief would be conditioned by much more input than the biblical authors had. For instance, my belief would be very much conditioned by theologians like Pierre Teilhard de Chardin, because Teilhard took for granted evolution. These authors didn't know anything about evolution at all. They would have a very static viewpoint."

During a five-day course in 1983, Mary had occasion to ask that same Diocesan expert whether changes in the Mass since 1961 might actually be resulting in a Mass that is something different than it was before the changes. To this question, he replied with a 2,500-word, stem-winding jaunt through theology and social custom before driving to the crux:

> "Everybody that I have ever seen who went back to a Latin Eucharist, walked away from there saying "Ah, it felt so good." If you come on over I'll give you a back rub sometime. That'll feel good too [laughter]. I don't know what it has to do with worship, to assist at a Eucharist. Get that on your tape recorder. To assist at a Eucharist in Latin when nobody understands Latin is a travesty on liturgy. I don't know of any other liturgist who will

---

98   One who claimed in The Messenger to have taught about five thousand Scripture sessions and classes.

say anything else. Why anybody would assist at a Eucharist in a language they cannot understand tells me they don't understand the liturgy or it's nothing but a show. I've got more important things to do than put on shows for people."

Belleville was one place where such musings from a Diocesan priest and scripture scholar wouldn't surprise anyone.

- And there was … The **Laity Synod of 1987**

… a particularly painful experience for Mary and Mary Ann. This was a Belleville Diocese gathering to produce a formal set of answers to be carried by representatives of the Diocese to a regional meeting and then to the World Synod of Bishops. Mary and Mary Ann hoped it might be an opportunity to advance prospects for the Latin Mass. They registered in advance (as required) and pre-pared for the 4 hour event, diligently pouring over the 10-page "Lineaments" document mailed out by the Diocese. On arriving at the large auditorium venue, they signed in and received name tags. A small number in the upper right corner designated each attendee's discussion small group. Mary and Mary Ann did not have the same number. The agenda called for four twenty-minute presentations, each one followed by five minutes to assemble into small groups of 8-10, twenty minutes of small group discussion, 5 minutes of summarizing and five minutes where all groups reported back to the full assembly. As the day unfolded, the scheme of the organizers became clear. The sessions were too short to allow for any meaningful input or discussion. The chairman in each group had been pre-determined by the organizers. Reports to the full session were incredibly brief. And most revealing of all, "known dissenters" had obviously been separated as much as possible across the small groups. Thus no small group would have a "dissenter" contingent sizable enough to force discussion of Tradition or the Latin Mass, and such issues would not be included in a report. The Belleville

Diocese Laity Synod had been programmed for the desired results. Mary and Mary Ann were discouraged, but not surprised.

- And there was … Belleville's dismissal of the **Papal Indult of 1988**[99]

   … The Bishop of Belleville's remarkable *refusal to act,* when formally "asked" by the Pope to be more generous in granting the Latin Mass to anyone who asked. Leadership in the Diocese, apparently determined to quash any resurgence of the Latin Mass and despite continued pleas from traditional Catholics like Mary, openly defied the Pope's wishes and did not act - nor provide any explanation - for six full years.

- And there was … The **National Shrine of Our Lady of the Snows**[100]

   … its influence as high-profile home to a parade of events like Bernstein's Mass, presented on the Altar at the Shrine's grand Outdoor Amphitheatre. The shrine also exerted its influence continually with educational programs of every sort. Take for instance "Journey to Wholeness" a 1989 conference of numerous workshops for divorced, separated, single, and widowed. Sponsored by the Belleville Diocese and developed in response to a Diocesan listening session held in 1987, the keynote speaker was Reverend Tom Jones, pastor of Emmanuel *Presbyterian* Church. Features included an interdenominational prayer service, candlelight reconciliation service, and a Eucharist celebrated by Belleville's Bishop.

---

99 Apostolic Letter "Ecclesia Dei" July 1988. Response of the Vatican to ordination of bishops by Archbishop Lefebvre. The request for Bishops to be more generous in granting the Latin Mass was a stated strategy to lure Catholics away from the SSPX Masses.

100 At 200 acres, one of the largest outdoor shrines in North America. Served by the Missionary Oblates of Mary Immaculate.

- And there were ... **Priests distracted from tending the flock**[101]

  ... spending more time away from their parishes. New training and development programs were one reason.[102] Belleville's Regional Catholic Leadership (RCL) program was one, created to develop priest's skills in communicating and managing change. The first RCL class, in 1989, required fourteen priests to commit 24 days over 18 months. Those fourteen were joined by fifty-six others for phase two ... four single day sessions. In addition to new training, priests were called to spend time in Diocesan support such as Priest Senate meetings (two-day meetings for about twenty priests at the Bishop's home), from which four or more Belleville Diocese priests would then be sent on to the annual five-day National Federation of Priest's Councils conference. And in 1987 the need for yet another conference apparently arose, this time for all priests in the Diocese. The first Convocation for Diocesan Priests (Belleville Diocese, that is) was held in French Lick, IN in 1987. The second, a five-day affair, convened in 1990 at Paducah, KY.

- And there were ... **Words and Images** arriving every Friday in The Messenger, official news-carrier for the Belleville Diocese. **A sampling:**

---

101 Exacerbated by a noticeable shortage of priests. As of 1983, discussion of parish clustering in the Belleville Diocese had already been going on for several years. In twenty years the number of priests had declined from 160 to 135. Seminarians had declined from 196 to 19. One priest was ordained for the Diocese of Belleville in 1983. There were no further ordinations scheduled until 1986. Compounding the problem, there was also a seemingly growing need for mental health treatment among the religious. New programs like the "House of Affirmation Inc." in St. Louis. Director Sister Kathleen M. Kelley S.N.D, said in a 1981 interview, "The problems of many of the center's clients developed during the 1970's when the structure of the Catholic Church radically changed." The facility operated as a co-educational environment with ten priests and ten nuns at a time. Program elements included psychodrama, yoga sessions, art therapy, and dancing with emphasized body awareness. "We want them to know they have a body," Sr. Kathleen said.

102 Prior to 1960, Mary was unaware of any training for priests which physically pulled them away from their assignments.

Social activism of every stripe

Take for instance an installment from a regular columnist[103] praising a movie whose main character, a female, discovers "life is too short to spend talking to walls and being her husband's lackey." The movie's heroine eventually found her full potential by leaving her husband, having an affair in a foreign country, and staying abroad with a new job. The lengthy column ended with the author's progressive summation, "Why do we get all this life, if we don't ever use it? We need to live it with passion."

Promotion of heterodox organizations and programs

Taize[104] garnered a generous spread, encouraging youth of the Belleville Diocese "who may feel boxed in by a God who is too predictable, who is, in short, more dead than alive" to attend Taize's Pilgrimage of Trust on Earth where they can "root their lives more deeply in a relationship with the "Pilgrim God."[105]

Endless innovations at Masses

Around the Diocese, from the cultural to the artistic. Messenger photos and articles conveyed details of new wrinkles ranging from the incorporation of an Indian purification ritual into an Ash Wednesday Children's Service at the Shrine, to a troop of young girls adorned in angel gowns - dancing on the altar in a special Mass celebrating School's Week.

---

103   First column by contributing writer Sister Barbara Mayer OSB: The Messenger, August 24, 1990.

104   Taize is a progressive, France-based ecumenical group of "brothers," both Catholic and Protestant. They recruited youth to contribute to "a coming springtime of the Church."

105   The Messenger 8/24/92, Taize's route for the young: meeting the unknown God.

CAPSTONE - THE SCANDAL OF 1993

The Diocese of Belleville, characterized by most as "rural" and tucked neatly into southern Illinois, probably seldom - if ever- had appeared in the L.A. Times before 1993. But on October 31st of that year, the Times made Belleville the subject of a full article. Some other news sources followed, but not many. The reason for the attention was sexual abuse of minors by members of the clergy. Belleville had just removed eight[106] priests and one deacon from active parish duty, in a span of five months, after investigating accusations[107] made against them. A brief firestorm of negative attention descended on the Diocese. Then it disappeared as quickly as it had appeared. Years later similar stories would unfold in dioceses with larger media markets, Boston most notably assuming the spotlight in 2003, and the problem[108] mushroomed nationally. The rest of the Church's history with this issue is well-documented.[109]

Yet looking back now, it is hard not to see little Belleville as a sort of Ground Zero, or a canary in the coal mine for the sexual abuse crisis in the Church. That raises questions. Why did the problem surface so early in Belleville? And why (with Belleville suddenly losing 11 out of 110 active priests) was the problem there so relatively large?

For the most part, faithful throughout the Belleville Diocese had been stunned, sad, embarrassed and angry.[110] Embers weren't immune from that angst, with one significant qualification. The one emotion an Ember didn't

---

106   Within just over a year, three more priests would be removed, making the total 11 by January of 1995.

107   Except for one instance, accusations alleged that the acts had happened between 1968 and 1983.

108   Our focus here is solely on the sexual abuse of minors by clergy, not to be confused with the much broader issue of all sexual misconduct within the Catholic clergy.

109   Though it is not all solved, even in 2020. As for Belleville, by 2002 fifteen priests had been removed.

110   Some anger was directed at the Bishop who, having just completed a lengthy term in Belleville, had now been promoted to Archbishop in Kansas City. Past Bishops weren't exempt either … as the story was getting headlines two priests came forward claiming they had gone to Bishops in the 1960's, 1970's and 1980's to report allegations and rumors about one of the priests who was eventually dismissed.

feel was surprise. To the Ember, the rip current surging through the Diocese for over twenty years had been too obvious. In hindsight, an Ember would suggest that Belleville arriving on the public scene earlier than most, and having a proportionately bigger problem than most, probably isn't such a mystery. Take a small and slightly isolated diocese, focus uncommon and unrelenting zeal on the "the spirit of Vatican II," and see what happens.

RAYS OF LIGHT

For tradition-minded Catholics, the Belleville Diocese has been a dark place for over fifty years. Even so, rays of light emerged from time to time. They didn't always last, but they did sometimes provide hope. And, just maybe those rays illuminated a path for others…

THE LOG CHURCH AND MONSIGNOR JEROME

Fifty three blocks west on Main Street from Belleville's town square a small group of people poured out the front door of St. Henry's Church. It was a gorgeous Saturday morning in September of 1994. This did not happen every Saturday morning. It occurred once a month, just as the bishop had allowed when the first-Saturday Mass started nine years back in '85. For nine years they asked the same bishop to allow the Latin Mass more often and on Sundays, but to no avail. Still, the group of 20-30 faithful kept coming to their first-Saturday Mass each month. As did their loyal priest, Monsignor Bauer. And there was Smitty still driving in from Mascoutah, serving the Mass with his cousin. The only change in almost a decade had been the organist. Mrs. Timmer was tragically killed in an auto accident just months after the Mass at St. Henry's had started.[111] Within weeks Divine Providence shone on the Mass again, bringing Gorman Rothlisberger to occupy her bench. Gorman fit in well and became a regular at lunch following the Mass.

---

111 Of all places, the accident occurred at the front entrance to Our Lady of the Snows Shrine. Her friends took some comfort from the fact that a priest was in the car behind her and was able to give her last rites before she died.

But recently a new bishop had arrived. The first-Saturday group was nervous, and chattering on the sidewalk outside church. No one knew how he would look upon their Latin Mass. Optimists thought there was a chance he would expand the Latin Mass, pessimists worried he might eliminate it. The group had reached out to their new shepherd even before boxes were unpacked at his official residence, but so far no word. They didn't have to wait long. The Messenger edition of September 16 carried the news - and surprised everyone. The new bishop was shutting down their first-Saturday Mass at St. Henry's. Well, technically he was transferring it ... from St. Henry's Church to "The Log Church" in Cahokia. BUT, he was also changing the day of the Mass to Sundays, and it would now be weekly. This was big news. After decades of pleading, on September 25th a Sunday Latin Mass was at last going to be celebrated in the Belleville Diocese.

As with the announcement of the St. Henry's Mass so many years before, Mary and her friends were elated. The location wasn't one they would have chosen, but progress is still progress - and they now had Sunday Mass. The Log Church, built in 1799, is reputed to be the oldest church west of the Allegheny Mountains. It's even listed as a National Historic Landmark. So on the bright side, it had a little bit of name recognition. And, at 32 feet by 72 feet, it was arguably the right size, an intimate chapel for this small group. The building was well-maintained for hosting historic tour groups and the occasional wedding or funeral. But there were two downsides. First, the Log Church is located in an area with one of the highest crime rates in the United States.[112] Second, in a Diocese sprawled across twenty eight counties and almost twelve thousand square miles, the log church sits at the extreme northwest corner of the diocese. A little over a mile to the west *or* to the north, and the Log Church would be in the Mississippi River. Bottom line: it is *very* out of the way for almost anyone in the Diocese, and it sits in a neighborhood many people think twice about entering.

---

112   www.neighborhoodscout.com

The Log Church – Cahokia, IL

Location of Log Church in Diocese

The new Sunday TLM at the Log Church was an early act in the eleven-year stay of Bishop Wilton Gregory.[113] Whether the intent of the bishop was to expand the Mass or constrain it – remains a fair question to ask; Bishop Gregory has periodically been a magnet for controversy. In any case, on Sunday, September 25, the operation previously located at St. Henry's Church, held its first Sunday Mass at the Log Church. Monsignor Bauer

---

113 Wilton Gregory served as bishop of the Belleville diocese from 1993 to 2004, and then was assigned to Atlanta. His name may be familiar to Catholics today as he is now the Archbishop of Washington D.C.

welcomed the faithful to their new home. Attendance surged a bit from the St. Henry's numbers, to forty or so.[114]

For those in the pews, this Sunday Mass represented a major change. Before that day, each of them had somehow found an answer to their own Sunday Mass Dilemma. Mary had been to Sunday Mass at Queen of the Holy Rosary in St. Louis since 1979. Mary Ann for a few years at St. Agatha's in St. Louis, where Smitty had begun to join her. And so on, down the line. Now all of them were making a major change, going to the Log Church for the most important act in their Catholic week. In so doing, they were sacrificing whatever sense of "parish" they may have found elsewhere. Now they were part of a "mission chapel," by definition only really existing for an hour or so every Sunday. For some, that can be a gut check. Others, of course, had been there before.

The Mass at the Log Church went off without hitch into the winter. But even before spring - when the attendees could stop wearing their winter gloves and scarves during Mass,[115] another change came their way. For the first time since most of them could remember, Monsignor Bauer didn't show up. His health had finally forced him to step aside from this assignment. In his place was a thin priest of medium height with gray hair who had volunteered to assume the role. Many of the mass-goers that morning didn't know the priest, but they had no reservations about one who could offer their Latin Mass. Mary and Russ most certainly did know him, though it had been years since they had seen Monsignor Jerome. They were thrilled to see him, especially in this situation. To see him here for a Latin Mass indicated his passion for tradition had persisted! Monsignor Jerome must have stayed on the path he appeared to be taking before he left St. Mary's Church so suddenly six years earlier. To Mary and Russ, it was a happy reunion with a man they

---

114 The actual number of attendees, which held up over the years, proved Mary's long-held contention that more Catholics would attend a Latin Mass on Sunday than had done so on Saturdays at St. Henry's. In addition, it is reasonable to assert that the numbers would be higher if not for the location. Mary spoke personally to many people over the years who would attend the Mass if it were located somewhere other than Cahokia.

115 A heating system hadn't yet been installed in the Log Church.

greatly respected. For Monsignor Jerome and the Sunday congregation at the Log Church, it was the beginning of good years together.

For those who attended the Log Church Mass through the late 1990's, one short stretch of time seems to stand out in their memories. On September 19, 1999, Monsignor Jerome stepped to the old oak lectern to deliver his Sunday morning homily. He had offered this Mass for over four years now and always gave meaningful sermons on relevant topics, doctrinally sound. His small flock was all ears as usual. Very quickly they sensed this sermon was something different. On that day Monsignor Harry Jerome presented Part One of a six-part series of homilies he titled "Why the Traditional Mass of the Roman Rite?" The six parts, delivered on consecutive Sundays, went together to explain what happened to the Old Mass between 1960 and 1999, and why that Mass - the Traditional Mass of the Roman Rite - was still far superior for a Catholic than the New Mass. It is notable that Monsignor Jerome ended the first and sixth parts with the same important guidance, "In any discussion you have with others who disagree with you about the Mass – IN ALL THINGS, CHARITY."

The individual parts of the series were scholarly, passionate dives into: the Constitution on the Sacred Liturgy (by the fathers of Vatican II), the Position of the Priest, the Suppression of the Offertory Prayer, the Latin Language, the Vernacular, and Ecumenism. When he finished the sixth part on October 24, those sitting in the pews knew they were looking at a very brave man. What they had heard was a pronouncement by a man making a stand for what he believed, and very ably defending it ... the kind of talk you would expect to hear from a Bishop John Fisher in England. Twenty years later they easily recall the memory. Many asked Monsignor Jerome for copies of the sermon series, and he graciously provided them the following Sunday.

A few months after that sixth sermon, in February of 2000, Monsignor Jerome was removed from his role at the Log Church. Those in the pews weren't told why. He was reassigned as pastor at Sacred Heart Catholic Church in Duquoin IL. It was his hometown, sixty five miles of two-lane highway out into southern Illinois. The sudden departure of Monsignor Jerome was the final straw for Mary and Russ at the Log Church. They headed back to St. Louis. Mary Ann and Smitty did the same.

The Log Church might remain a ray of light in the Belleville Diocese, but without a few of its regulars.

POOR CLARES

A discussion of rays of light in Belleville would be incomplete without mention of the Poor Clares. This is an order of contemplative, cloistered nuns founded in 1212 by St. Clare under the guidance and inspiration of St. Francis of Assisi. According to The Messenger, the Bishop of Belleville invited them to establish a presence. He announced upon their arrival in 1986 that they were beginning their "service of prayer and penance for the needs of the people of the Diocese of Belleville." The diocese immediately raised funds for a new monastery and in 1989 the nuns moved into their new facility just west of St. Henry's Church, set back from Main Street on wooded property once occupied by the Diocese's seminary. Visitors are welcome at the monastery to pray, adore the Eucharist and attend morning Mass – all on the public side of a wall that separates them from the cloistered nuns. In recent years, Mary has enjoyed visiting on Sunday afternoons for vespers, the rosary, and then benediction by a visiting Oblate priest.

The Poor Clares are without question a ray of light in the Belleville Diocese.

GANG OF NINE

Most of us have experiences in our past that almost seem surreal, but they most certainly happened. Mary had one of these, and Mary Ann was with her. The two ladies received a very unusual invitation from a priest friend of theirs. They were invited, by word of mouth only, to arrive at St. Augustine's Catholic Church in Belleville on a particular Thursday evening at 7:00 p.m. for a Traditional Latin Mass. They were not to tell anyone else about it.

On that Thursday evening, the two met fifteen minutes early in the parking lot behind St. Augustine's Church and made their way up the sidewalk to the side door as they had been instructed. It was not locked and they walked in. There was no one else in the Church. Unsure exactly what to do, they quietly walked around to the back, stepped into a pew, and opened their missals to pray. Just before 7:00 the silence was delicately broken by the shuffling of feet. From the sacristy on the left, they saw a priest in all black attire with white collar walk to the side of the sanctuary, genuflect, and proceed to the first pew. That priest was followed by another, and another and another … until seven priests were in the first pew, four on the right of the center aisle and three on the left. None of the priests acknowledged the two ladies sitting in back in the church. A bell rang and from the same sacristy came a priest in full vestments, followed by one male server in black cassock and white surplice. The Latin Low Mass followed, consistent with Mary's yellow-paged 1962 Missal. When the Mass was completed, all the priests returned to the sacristy. There were no greetings for the ladies, no acknowledgment that they were even present. Mary and Mary Ann left as they had arrived, but stunned by what they just witnessed. Nine priests had attended the Mass, one was the celebrant. Some, but not all, of their faces were familiar. From their priest friends they eventually learned just a bit more about that Mass. The Mass was a regular event, once a month, though the location would vary. And there were nine priests, all from the Belleville Diocese who attended. That was it. Mary and Mary Ann were left to wonder about anything else, including why they had been allowed to witness such a private moment for these priests. One thing they did take away was knowledge that some priests in the diocese were staying sharp with their skills in saying the Latin Mass. This gave them hope. They saw even more hope in this new evidence of more priests than they had previously known in the diocese who loved the Latin Mass. At the same time, it was a sad reminder of the silent suffering being endured by priests in a diocese that kept the Latin Mass under its thumb.

Both of them agreed that maybe they could hope more tradition-minded Catholics existed in the diocese and elsewhere, than they had dared dream lately. In the final analysis, they surmised that some - or even all - of those takeaways were why the priests had invited them to Mass on a Thursday night.

EMBERS EPILOGUE

SSPX in St. Louis and Beyond

While Mary and Russ were at the Log Church (1994-1999), Queen of the Holy Rosary Chapel was on the move. The Society purchased a church in 1997, formerly home to the Catholic Ruthenian Rite in Downtown St. Louis. Following extensive renovation, the new St. Mary's Assumption Church opened on Dolman Street in the Lafayette Square neighborhood. Mary was overjoyed on her first visit. From communion rail to tabernacle to crucifix, every meaningful feature was there. Creaky wooden floors and aging straight-back pews completed the traditional wonder. Mary couldn't help thinking as she had twenty five years ago in the hotel conference room off Highway 44, "I'm home."

Queen of the Holy Rosary Academy reclaimed its auditorium. One classroom was renovated into a chapel for the students. The school continues its mission of solid K-8 education with an unapologetically traditional Catholic underpinning.

Beyond St. Louis, the SSPX has continued its mission full force. They now have almost 700 priests and serve the faithful in over 70 countries around the world.[116] They operate six seminaries, the largest being St. Thomas Aquinas Seminary in Dilwyn, Virginia with over seventy seminarians. Much has also happened in the past fifteen years regarding SSPX's relationship with Rome. In particular, in 2009 the Vatican formally lifted the excommunications

---

116   According to Wikipedia ... If the Society's canonical situation were to be regularized, it would be the Catholic Church's 4th largest society of apostolic life

previously levied on the four Bishops consecrated by Archbishop Lefebvre at Econe in 1988. The Vatican also went on to formally affirm Sacraments performed by SSPX priests such as Confession and Marriage.

The priestly Society of St. Pius X and the Vatican are still at odds on certain doctrinal issues, and there is no sign these will be resolved anytime soon. Here's why: beyond merely the preservation of the true priesthood and of the sacrifice of the Mass (which SSPX still does not trust the Roman authority or individual bishops to sustain), is also a more general matter. From SSPX's perspective, there exists a crisis of faith, grounded in errors of Vatican II, and reflected in ecumenism and liberalism. Unless backed up by Catholic doctrine in its full integrity, preserving just the traditional liturgy would be seen as pointless. Meanwhile, clarifications from Rome regarding SSPX's status are painting a more unified picture, and SSPX continues its growth and geographical expansion.

TLM on the march

Today, the Traditional Latin Mass and other traditional practices are far more accessible for Catholics than they have been at any time in the last fifty years. This is due, in great part, to Pope Benedict XVI's 2007 apostolic letter titled Summorum Pontificum which significantly loosened restrictions on the Latin Mass. St. Louis is a poster-child for the upward trend.

Imagine you live across from the New St. Louis Cathedral, which is near the center of the St. Louis metropolitan area. On a Sunday morning, you have the ability to choose from Traditional Latin Masses at five different churches, four of them within five miles of your front door. Three of the four are diocesan churches (one being the Latin Mass Oratory of Ss. Gregory & Augustine), and the fourth is St. Mary's Assumption (SSPX). Also among the four is St. Francis de Sales Church, a magnificent building known as the Cathedral of South St. Louis, staffed by priests of the Institute of Christ the King Sovereign Priest. The fifth TLM is found thirty five miles northwest and serves a growing suburban area in St. Charles County.

St. Louis is also home to a vibrant Juventutem chapter, started in 2016. This group, youth under the age of 35 devoted to the Traditional Latin Mass, has brought its beautiful sacred music to dozens of churches around the St. Louis area - introducing the Latin Mass to thousands of local Catholics of all ages. A new St. Louis chapter of Una Voce started in 2020 as a result of Juventutem's success.

Demand for the Latin Mass may not be met as robustly elsewhere in the U.S. as it is in St. Louis, but the march continues. In addition to SSPX, many TLM churches are served by priests from FSSP, formally a "society of apostolic life" in the Catholic Church. As noted earlier, FSSP originated in 1988 when a number of priests split from SSPX in the aftermath of the Econe consecrations. There are now over 300 FSSP priests serving in 15 countries and 142 dioceses. FSSP priests are answerable only to the pope (rather than the local bishop) in operational matters. Another source of priests who celebrate the TLM is the Institute of Christ the King Sovereign Priest. The Institute, started in 1990 in Africa and given the status of pontifical right in 2008, now has over 100 priests and serves in nine U.S. states.

Today in the Belleville Diocese

In the year 2020, the only public Traditional Latin Mass available to a Catholic in the Belleville Diocese is on Sunday morning at 9:00 a.m. at the Log Church in Cahokia. Twenty five years have come and gone since the Latin Mass was moved there from St. Henry's on Main Street. Two bishops have led the diocese since then, and have periodically received requests for an expansion of the Latin Mass to other locations and to weekdays. The requests have either been denied or ignored.

Mary and Russ

Mary and Russ never left St. Mary's Assumption after returning there in 2000. Russ passed away in 2013. His Requiem High Mass was held at St. Mary's Assumption and the funeral caravan processed back to Belleville where he rests. Mary celebrated her ninetieth birthday in 2019.

And yes, Mary is aware that there is a new bishop moving into Belleville. She hasn't decided whether she will write a letter to him.

Peggy and Ed

Peggy is going strong in her eighties. She still belongs to St.Mary Assumption Church and helps out there - though a little less than in years past. More of her time goes to her kids and grandkids. Ed passed away in 2008, but not before an important change in his life. Shortly before he died, Ed decided to become Catholic. The person who won him over was a priest from the La Sallette Mission in south St. Louis, the man who never lost contact with a family that walked into his chapel back in 1973. The Prior at St. Mary's Assumption has asked Peggy to write a history of the church and the school. Good choice. No one could know the whole story like Peggy knows it.

Mary Ann and Smitty

Mary Ann and Smitty had options when they left the Log Church, but the decision wasn't difficult. The grandchildren helped, or at least the two oldest children of their daughter Donna. They were twins, boy and girl and they had just begun school at Queen of the Holy Rosary Academy. Donna and her husband Phil were becoming regulars at the Chapel, and Mary Ann and Smitty followed. Smitty, always magnetic, became a busy and popular member of the Church. When he passed away in January of 2004, a remarkable number of friends braved icy conditions to fill the Church on Dolman Street. Phil and Donna became very active at the Church and school, integral parts of both for years to come. The twins went on to commit their lives to the Church. Julie is a nun in the Dominican order in Fanjeaux, France. Peter was ordained to the priesthood in 2017 and now serves the mission chapel in Albuquerque from the SSPX priory in Phoenix, AZ. Mary Ann Winter - wife, mother, grandmother, and active Traditional Catholic - died in April of 2017. From a pew in their beloved old church, Mary prays for the soul of her stalwart ally and great friend.

Monsignor Harry Jerome

Monsignor Jerome went on to lead Sacred Heart Church in Du Quoin Illinois as pastor for almost ten years after leaving the Log Church. He passed away in 2010. This was a man who had been through a lot in his last twenty five years. Back when Mary first met him in 1984, he seemed committed to "the spirit of Vatican II." Then he lived through an apparent full-blown change of heart and mind. And to a reasonable observer, it appears that Monsignor Jerome was persecuted, not once but twice, for the crime of behaving in a traditional manner. The first instance was at St. Mary's Church in 1988 where he was pressured by progressive parishioners, likely contributing to his sudden removal as pastor. Then the second instance at the Log Church in 2000, where his six-part pronouncement of the virtues of the Traditional Mass of the Roman Rite appears to have been grounds for dismissing him from the Log Church Sunday Mass. As a consolation, Monsignor Jerome was permitted to say the Latin Mass publicly once per month at Sacred Heart Church. He may have said it more often privately, but no one seems to know for sure.

This priest was more than a ray of light. His journey was that of an Ember … a priestly Ember, in the Belleville Diocese no less. He led in the way he felt necessary to give hope, opportunity, and needed direction to faithful Catholics under his care. This gentle, thoughtful priest did this despite great personal peril and he paid a steep price, in this lifetime.

EMBER GEMS

The Ember stories are replete with good takeaways, and some will be especially valuable for the work ahead in Part Four. I hope you carry forward gems such as these:

- Catholics have indeed been deprived of many elements of the Church's pre-Vatican II Tradition.

  - Much confusion has been sown regarding official teachings. To overcome this, laypersons often have no choice but to seek out answers on their own.

  - Certain truths may fall out of popular favor, but they are still the teachings of the one, true Church.

  - Progressives play hardball in implementing their desired changes in the Church. Recognizing this, it is prudent to question "innovations."

  - If a Catholic is not comfortable with the level of reverence given to Sacred Tradition at his parish, it may be necessary to "shop" for a different parish - or even diocese.

- Traditional Church practices never died. They were guarded and nurtured by Embers across the globe. Their popular resurgence, while never guaranteed, should not surprise anyone. They are certainly not to be feared.

- Personal decisions about one's Catholic faith are not always easy, and they are not always pain-free.

- There are good, holy, tradition-loving priests among the clergy. They need our support in many ways. And Catholics seeking reliable spiritual growth must find them, even if the search is difficult.

- God really does provide answers, if we pray hard, listen harder, and use the intelligence He gave us. God also chooses, for reasons known only to Him, unexpected people to carry out His will, on His schedule. We must not become discouraged or afraid. Just remain faithful.

Having gleaned what we can about Catholic Tradition looking back over time, let us turn to the present day – and to our futures.

PART FOUR:
FAMILY REUNION –
IN HEAVEN?

*We now know how Catholic Tradition was kept from us, and
we understand a little more about what it is.
How do we help our children (and ourselves) get to Heaven?*

CHAPTER 8:

WHY YOUR CHILDREN WON'T GET TO HEAVEN

So why won't Johnny or Suzie get to heaven? We acknowledged early on that none of us can say with certainty whether he will or won't. At most, we can know (or suspect) that Johnny, by his actions and beliefs, is taking risks with his soul right now. Only when he gets to the gates, will he find out whether he took too many.

What "risks" are we talking about?

Let's make sure we are on the same page, by getting specific. We are talking now about *behaviors* and *beliefs,* but not extreme ones such as first-degree murder, or atheism, or little white lies. Most Catholic adults would easily agree that those are obviously either disqualifying or survivable.

The behaviors and beliefs of interest to us are those that Johnny and other nominal Catholics appear to have a harder time identifying as risky. Examples:

- Skipping Mass on Sunday

- Avoiding regular confession

- Not performing some type of penance regularly

- Disrespecting one's parents

- Not attending Mass on Holy Days of Obligation

- Not actively encouraging one's children in their Catholic faith

- Marrying a divorced person, if the previous marriage has not been annulled
- Condoning same-sex marriage
- Participating in, or supporting abortion
- Receiving Holy Communion while openly cohabitating outside of marriage
- Holding and/or promoting the idea that all religions are equally good
- Holding that Christ is not truly present in the Holy Eucharist
- Holding that God is all-merciful, that He does not also impose justice
- Denying the existence of hell, or claiming it is empty
- Condoning or participating in artificial contraception
- Promoting Communist or Socialist philosophies

Important Assertion:

Johnny would not agree that everything on this list is risky behavior for a Catholic.He would argue with one or more, perhaps placing conditions on his position.

But Johnny would be wrong, because every one of the behaviors and beliefs on the long list above is in direct opposition to the clear teachings of Christ and the Catholic faith. And our conditions don't matter.

REFRESHER – TRADITION & DEPOSIT OF THE FAITH

How can the claim be made, so matter-of-factly, that every one of the behaviors and beliefs on the long list above is in direct opposition to Church teaching? The Sacred Deposit of the Faith tells us so.

Most Catholics today would have a hard time explaining what is meant by the Sacred Deposit of the Faith (a safe bet, I think). I'll be the first to concede that for most of my life I would have struggled. One day I discovered it, and then other terms like Tradition and Magisterium followed.

*The "Sacred Deposit" of the faith consists of **Sacred Scripture** +
Sacred Tradition. In addition, the bishops working with the Pope
are responsible for authentic interpretation over time, which is
called the **Magisterium**. Together these three are considered the
whole teaching of the Faith, sometimes collectively referred to as
the **Deposit of the Faith**.*[117]

We are all familiar with Scripture (another safe bet, I hope), but probably less so with that Tradition piece. Until recently, I had made the common mistake of assuming Catholic Tradition was like any other "tradition": customs we had adopted and carry forward, but not exactly consequential in the whole scheme of things. As it turns out, the Catechism of the Catholic Church (CCC) says Tradition is much more than that:

*"Through **Tradition**, the Church, in her doctrine, life, and worship
perpetuates and transmits to every generation what she herself
is, all that she believes."*

That made me take note, but *really* surprising was the level of importance then assigned to Tradition by the CCC:

*"Both Scripture and Tradition must be accepted and honored
with equal sentiments of devotion and reverence."*

Catholic teaching places Tradition on a pedestal next to Sacred Scripture! THAT is a call to attention.

One more notable thought from the CCC: all the faithful are entitled to *all* of Sacred Catholic Tradition.

Key takeaway:

Sacred Tradition is tremendously important for each of us in understanding fully the exact teaching of the Catholic Church.

---

117 Gleaned from the Catechism of the Catholic Church (CCC), which is fairly understandable for ordinary Catholics (don't be afraid of it!). Articles 50-95 deal with Deposit of the Faith.

In the case of our list above, every example runs counter to clear teaching in the Deposit of the Faith.

It follows that Johnny is taking risk.

Why is he doing that?

In many cases (I would guess most cases) because he does not really know what Church teaching is, and – just as importantly - why the teaching is what it is. He cannot know, because he was denied access to Sacred Tradition.

> **Assertion:**
>
> The primary reason Johnny cannot recognize behaviors or beliefs that run counter to the clear teachings of the Church is that he has never had access to the full Deposit of the Faith, especially all of the Church's Sacred Tradition.

INHERITANCE DENIED

Any baptized Catholic has the right to every bit of official Church Tradition that our ancestors have developed and passed forward. It is our rightful inheritance, as the Catechism points out. Yet the experiences of the Embers in Chapters Two, Three and Four demonstrate the extremes to which the Church went in attempting to extinguish its own Tradition pre-dating 1965. In hindsight, it is surreal how quickly and universally the Church moved to purge its past. By the year 2020, we now have several generations (Johnny's included) who have lived childhood into adulthood with no access to a large portion of their rightful inheritance. Without knowing the whole of Tradition, Johnny cannot know the whole of the Deposit of the Faith. Without knowing the Deposit of the Faith, Johnny has one eye covered in trying to distinguish risky behaviors and beliefs, those that pull him away from heaven.

THE BISHOP MADE HIM DO IT

In saying that Johnny was denied his rightful inheritance, are we pointing to any persons in particular? Yes, primarily to the bishops.[118] They run the Church and have been entrusted by God to defend the Faith handed to them by the apostles. The bishops participated together in Vatican II, produced its documents, and oversaw the implementation of its changes. They conducted Vatican II as a united body, so it should not be surprising that every bishop subsequently supported its implementation. Even if a bishop was inclined not to wholeheartedly support the council's implementation, he would most likely do so anyway - knowing that anything less would be met with fury from his brethren. This reality was confirmed by the treatment Archbishop Marcel Lefebvre received from his fellow bishops.

At the local level, Bishops exert total control, so the unity among bishops following Vatican II virtually ensured that Johnny, no matter where he lived on planet Earth, would be surrounded by the post-Vatican II Church. Anyone doubting the control of a bishop over his diocese needs look no further than the Diocese of Belleville, still suffocating the Traditional Latin Mass even today.

Assertion:

Johnny also received false or misleading support and guidance from those he trusts, contributing to his inability to recognize behaviors or beliefs that run counter to the clear teachings of the Church.

THE PARISH PRIEST

It was not unusual, over the past fifty years, for Johnny to receive guidance from his parish priest that conflicted with the Deposit of the Faith.[119] We saw this shortly after Vatican II when Mary sought answers about the status

---

118 As we know, archbishops, cardinals and even the Pope are bishops.

119 Of course the extent of this has varied widely, depending on individual priests .

of the Latin Mass from various priests. The teachings of Humanae Vitae and many others were similarly misrepresented. How to explain this?

First, the priests of the Catholic Church are the products of the seminaries. Many seminaries, more specifically the teachers in them, took very progressive turns even before Vatican II. We have many excellent, pious priests in the Church, but our seminaries have also produced a bumper crop of misguided priests who have veered from the Deposit of the Faith anchored in Tradition.

Second, we find answers in the very nature of the relationship between the parish priest and his bishop. At ordination, a priest vows obedience to his bishop. That fact alone may be answer enough – but there is more to understand. Put simply, a diocesan priest, who has committed his life to his vocation and dedicated many years to his own education, is quite beholden to his bishop. The priest receives and holds his parish assignment at the pleasure of his bishop, and from the parish or bishop flow virtually all his living arrangements. Cross your bishop, expect reprisal.[120] Fittingly then, most priests will follow the leadership of their bishop. And, as described above, the bishops were in lockstep following Vatican II. As we learned in the Ember stories, some priests not philosophically aligned with their bishops have endured stress levels over the past fifty years that we laity can't truly comprehend. Persecution of tradition-minded parish priests continues today.

Given all this, it should not be surprising that Johnny's parish priest may have actually been an obstacle to Johnny ever coming to know the Deposit of the Faith, and Tradition in particular.

THE FELLOW FAITHFUL

We may like to think that Johnny's fellow lay Catholics played no role in the sudden burying of Tradition. If only that were true. We contributed on multiple fronts:

---

120 Worst case, maybe out of a job. A lighter sentence is transfer to a less desirable or smaller parish in the Diocese. This has been a common punishment levied on tradition-leaning priests by their progressive bishops.

- Even among lay Catholics who did not agree with their bishops' departure from Tradition, most still complied. A reasonable explanation is that Catholics, especially those born before 1960, were raised to be obedient. While that is an admirable Catholic virtue, it hasn't helped Johnny.[121]

- Adult Catholics in the pews in the 1960's and 1970's watched the Catholic Mass dissolve toward Protestantism and either cheered it, or stayed quiet.

- Over these many years, parents continued sending their children to Catholic grade schools, high schools and colleges … knowing they were taught religion unmoored from Tradition. Worse yet, children often return home and convert parents, rather than parents correcting their children.

We should by now agree it is possible that Johnny is not able to fully recognize the real risks he is taking. And based on how this has come to be, we may concede that – to a great degree – it might not be Johnny's fault. Even so, we must acknowledge a dangerous trait that *would* actually be Johnny's fault – should it surface.

INTELLECTUAL HUBRIS

By intellectual hubris, I mean considering oneself smarter than others. In everyday life, behaving this way can irritate those others, but wouldn't normally be catastrophic. This cannot be said if the "other" is God. Human intelligence is infinitely microscopic compared to that of angels. Angelic intelligence is, in turn, infinitely microscopic next to God's. Considering, then, the massive chasm between our intelligence and God's, dare any of us consider our own judgement superior to His Deposit of the Faith? I'm an ordinary Catholic layperson so can't say, but some things just *feel* like intellectual hubris. For instance:

---

121 A truly ponder-worthy statement on this point: "For it is a master-stroke of Satan to get Catholics to disobey the whole of Tradition in the name of obedience." An Open Letter to Confused Catholics by Archbishop Marcel Lefebvre.

- Modernist theology (like teachings of the diocesan scholar Mary so often encountered)

- The cafeteria Catholic mindset (discussed later)

There are more and I am not judging any particulars here, but a reminder about humility never hurts.

SO WHY IS JOHNNY TAKING RISKS?

To some extent, the deck has been stacked against Johnny. But he is a thinking grown-up, so why would he be taking such risks? Three explanations seem plausible:

- He has simply never considered whether certain actions or beliefs might be wrong.

- He knows that the Church says a behavior or belief is wrong, but doesn't fear the consequences enough to steer clear.

- He believes, wrongly, that the Church says a particular behavior or belief is okay, because someone he trusts gave him bad support or guidance.

1. **"I never thought about it"**

    How could a Catholic have ended up here? Maybe he was baptized and never practiced the faith. In any case, he is seriously unaware of basic tenets of the Catholic faith. I have little to offer and will not dwell on it since I contend (or at least hope) that only a small percentage of our fellow Catholics are in this situation.

2. **"I know, but ... "**

    In this situation, Johnny knows the whole Deposit of the Faith and is making a conscious decision to do something he knows is opposed to the Church's Truth. It would seem obvious Johnny will be held accountable. How he got here I am not sure, but my first thought is that, despite claims to the contrary, Johnny is not familiar enough with the whole Deposit of the Faith.

3. "I have it on good authority that I am fine"

This brings us to what I believe explains the vast majority of risk-taking by Johnny and other Catholics in the world today: Someone Johnny trusts gave him bad support or guidance. These "trusted authorities" could be theologians or fellow laypersons, but in most cases are probably clergy. We can't know whether Johnny will eventually be held personally responsible for following guidance received from his priest or bishop, but the looming uncertainty of this situation is flat-out troubling.

Many years ago, amid the upheaval in the Church in the 1970's and 1980's, deferring entirely to the clergy may have been the only safe haven for many good Catholics.[122] I fear that approach may be less credible today, and here is why:

We Catholics today have information that our parents did not. In fact, we have mountains of easy-to-understand facts and data that tell us the last fifty years in the Catholic Church have been an unmitigated disaster. For instance:

- *As of 2019, only thirty one percent (31%) of self-described Catholics believe in the real presence of Christ in the Eucharist.*[123]

- *Catholics in the pews, vocations, baptisms, children in Catholic schools, Catholic marriages ... all down in a range from forty percent (40%) to seventy percent (70%) in just sixty years.*[124]

---

122 In the Ember stories were many good Catholics who decided to obey the direction given them by any Church authority, in the belief that if they [clergy] proved wrong, then they will pay the price. Russ (Mary's husband) held that belief originally.

123 Pew Research Center. "What Americans Know About Religion". Survey conducted 4-19, February 2019.

124 Center for Applied Research in the Apostolate. https://cara.georgetown.edu/frequently-requested-church-statistics/

However one looks at it, the growth and springtime of the Catholic Church promised by Vatican II has not happened. Results are obviously quite the opposite, and it would be hard to attribute these outcomes to anything other than the leadership of those who have transformed the Church over the last fifty years. That is my point of concern for Johnny.

In the face of overwhelming evidence of decline in the Catholic Church, will Johnny be able to plead ignorance? Can he possibly blame an authority he could easily have recognized as flawed? I cannot help but think of Mary's frequent use of Matthew 9:16, "By their fruits you will know them."

The fruits, in Johnny's case, are the results of the post-Vatican II Catholic Church and its leaders, under whom Johnny learned the Faith and lived his life (assuming he has continued to practice the faith). At some point, is Johnny responsible for continuing to follow the leaders he follows?

CAFETERIA CATHOLICISM

Most of us know someone who fits the description of a "cafeteria Catholic." This person might belong to group #1 or group #2 above. The cafeteria Catholic can't quite bring himself to subscribe to all of the teachings of the Catholic Faith. There is one (or more) teaching that just doesn't work for him, and for whatever reason he will not comply.[125] By definition, this represents an on-the-fence mentality toward the Catholic faith. Is this a risk worth taking? I hesitate to answer that before stopping to think about God's view of commitment...

IN OR OUT

One more line of thinking warrants mention, though a Catholic who is fully tuned in to the Deposit of the Faith probably knows this well. To Johnny, this may sound like a foreign language. The following two scripture passages strike at a serious point about getting to heaven:

---

125 In essence, the cafeteria Catholic is Protestant ("some, but not all"). By denying a principal doctrine, the individual is aligning with a heresy that either withers in time or becomes a separate religion. [Hilaire Belloc]

"I know thy works; thou art neither cold nor hot. I would that thou wert cold or hot. But because thou art lukewarm, and neither cold nor hot, I am about to vomit thee out of my mouth." Apocalypse, 3: 15-16

"He who eats my flesh and drinks my blood has life everlasting and I will raise him up on the last day ... From this time many of his disciples turned back and went about without him." John, 6:54 ... John, 6:65

This is simple but huge. Jesus made it clear that God expects us to be all-in. Anything less just doesn't work. (I find it particularly unnerving that lukewarm gets special mention as "not good enough".)

A sermon given recently by a local priest also addressed the "all-in" point:

Hold out both hands. Imagine in your right hand you are holding all the worldly goods (physical assets) you have accumulated during your life. In your left hand are the spiritual goods (graces) you have accumulated. A common human desire is to try to maximize as much as possible the pile of those worldy goods in your right hand, while juuuuust getting enough in your left hand to make it into Heaven. Now ... If you desired Heaven more than anything (or just feared Hell more than anything) wouldn't you do the exact opposite ... accumulate just enough worldly goods to make it through life, while piling up as many spiritual goods as possible?

TAKING STOCK

Why won't your children get to heaven? We can only say that IF they don't, it will be because they took too many risks, knowingly or unknowingly. They weren't all-in (enough).

We have sized up the problem, but we haven't solved anything. Maybe, just maybe, getting to this point has been necessary before we can begin to believe that brighter days are within reach for Johnny. Chapter Nine is for those of us who want to help him.

CHAPTER 9:
FAMILY REUNION IN HEAVEN (?)

You hope your children get to heaven, where you hope to be awaiting them. Johnny, God love him, appears to be taking risks that jeopardize the reunion. Can you help him recognize those risks, and maybe even adjust course? Yes, if you can usher him back to Catholicism as defined by the full Deposit of the Faith, including Sacred Tradition.

ALL ABOUT ATTITUDE

Success will rely on communicating effectively - and this depends on Johnny's general attitude at any given moment. Consider three general categories in which his attitude may fall:

A. **"Talk to the hand."**

   If Johnny has adopted this attitude, he has shut himself off from conversation about many touchy things, *especially* religion. You know from experience that raising the subject of faith with him will lead to argument or silence.

B. **"Tell me more."**

   Johnny does not seek out discussion of religion, but is somewhat open to it. He may be a nominal Catholic right now, but does at times wonder whether, or how, faith might one day mean more to him.

C. "Not now"

Johnny is not thinking about the Catholic faith (or any religion) right now. In fact, mention of it probably catches him off-guard. He is not one to raise the topic nor would he appear particularly interested in discussing it, because he is preoccupied with other things - temporal things, earthly things, material things - as are the people he spends time with.

"TALK TO THE HAND"

If Johnny, for whatever reason(s), absolutely refuses to entertain any discussion of faith, then options may be limited. He claims not to believe in God; believes there is too much corruption in any organized religion; is certain that all religion is just a crutch for weak people, etc., etc. Of course, one should always seek direction from a competent, Tradition-conscious priest who may have recommendations. But no matter the bleakness of the current situation, remember that with God ALL things are possible. For your part, there are at least two daily actions by which you can contribute to the cause.

First, pray - every day, specifically for the *full* conversion of your child. Mary (from the Ember stories) would recommend the Fatima Prayer for Conversions and the Memorare. Draw strength from knowing that you are not alone in this situation.

Second, always set good example. We've been told since the day we first became parents that our children are watching what we do. In fact, the little ones prove this at the most embarrassing times - like when four-year old Johnny used that bad word in a crowded grocery store checkout line. At any age, they are still watching. Recently I recalled for my mother a decision she made in 1988, when she turned the car around mid-trip and returned home, purely on a matter of principle. At the time, I felt she had ruined a big day for a ridiculous reason. But her stand was on an important moral issue. I have never forgotten it, and I hope I would have the courage to do the same today. We just cannot know when one action of ours will make an impact on others.

Lastly, never stop looking for signs of a seemingly cold heart beginning to thaw in your child. A talk-to-the-hand attitude may shift at any time - especially when major life events take place. As we move on to other attitudes, know that the actions suggested above are beneficial in every case.

"TELL ME MORE"

Suppose Johnny will talk, despite not being enthusiastic about his faith. Open ears and eyes are signs of a truly hopeful situation. Here again, always seek the advice of a competent, Tradition-conscious priest who may have recommendations for you about how to approach your child. But in any case, there are various actions you can take and suggestions you can make, whenever opportunity knocks with Johnny. For instance, you might advise him to:

- Sign on for one hour of Eucharistic Adoration at a local church ... say every two weeks, if at all possible at a time of day when the chapel is quiet (middle-of-the-night may seem extreme, but the solitude – and the effort to get there - can be very rewarding). What should he do there? Just sit quietly, ask for help of whatever kind he feels in need, and listen. Of course, he can pray formally or read, but even that isn't necessary – especially at first. God just wants to be invited. He will do the rest. One hour, every two weeks, no homework. If Johnny is genuinely curious about how faith can affect his life, this is a low-price ticket to check it out.

- Start a small daily commitment to God. Perhaps a quick read at night (My Daily Bread one-page reflections can be good). Or a morning prayer at the bathroom mirror (Morning Offering is tried-and-true). Or just five minutes of closed-eyes reflection after lunch, before his afternoon gets rolling.

- Find and read a book about a saint. Better yet, sample many books in search of a saint with whom he really connects. He will discover how gigantic the universe of saints really is, how different the saints are, and the depth of their virtues. (By the way, because you know Johnny, you might consider researching the saints yourself and then steering him toward those likely to pique his interest.) Suggestions from Mary's home library might include:

    - St. John Vianney

    - St. Joan of Arc

    - St. Isaac Jogues

    - St. Therese of Lisieux

    - St. Thomas More

    - St. Catherine of Siena

    - St. Francis of Assisi

- Undertake a quick research project (Google may be sufficient), on one of the following topics. These subjects can ignite curiosity and are teaming with elements of Catholic Tradition.

    - Our Lady of Fatima (the Marian apparition for our time)

    - Humanae Vitae (15 easy-to-read pages that shocked the Catholic world)

    - Eucharistic miracles (Christ's amazing gifts to today's doubting Thomases)

- Join a Catholic organization and be active. Make it one that is not primarily social, one focused on charitable acts, such as the St. Vincent DePaul Society.

Any of these actions, done with an open heart and mind, can energize a dormant soul. Tell Johnny it is perfectly fine to pace himself, but to be persistent - God will reward an interest that proves genuine. Eventually God will unveil for Johnny how He matters, how the Catholic faith will make a difference in his life and in his dealings with the world around him. Johnny will find that being a nominal Catholic will simply not be enough for him anymore.

Sooner or later, it will be advisable for Johnny to team with an excellent confessor and, if he wishes, a spiritual director. Finding a confessor and director with whom he makes a solid connection is no small task, and he needs to use all means at his disposal in searching.[126] There is a point to be emphasized here. Recall our most important goal ... that Johnny recognize the risks that may obstruct him in getting to heaven. As long as Johnny finds a solid, Tradition-minded priest to guide him, then we ought to be confident that he is going the right direction. But only by ensuring that Tradition is included in his development, can we know that Johnny is learning the whole Deposit of the Faith - and that he has the tools he needs to recognize risky behavior and beliefs.

"NOT NOW"

Last but not least is the child who is simply too tied up in living life to bother with religion. This version of Johnny is not necessarily opposed to Catholicism, or to religion in general. He just does not think about it. He does not see it as sufficiently relevant to the challenges he is busy slaying every day in the real world. My guess is that the majority of our Johnnies out there, the nominal Catholics who are taking unnecessary risks and whom we want to help, fit this description. But is it possible to get through to them?

By definition, we know their attitude is different than the two cases above. They will not automatically repel any approach, as would the "Talk to the Hand" group. But they are not as receptive to exploratory actions as the "Tell me more" group can be. If Johnny is in the "Not now" group, a more nuanced approached may be required. He is independent, with little tolerance for being preached to. But he is not opposed to ideas, if given space

---

126 Dr. Taylor Marshall presents helpful suggestions regarding how to search for a spiritual director at https://taylormarshall.com/2013/08/001-how-to-find-a-spiritual-director-podcast.html (min 6:45-15:00)

WHY YOUR CHILDREN WON'T GET TO HEAVEN

to process them on his own schedule. Thoughts and suggestions most likely to intrigue him are those he perceives as related to his current challenges and concerns.

Understanding our "Not now" child this way, what actions might we take to reach him, to help him understand the risks we believe he is taking with his soul? First recall that every action outlined in the "Talk to the hand" section above is perfectly suited for this. Then we commit to meeting Johnny on his own turf, with thought-provoking information on issues relevant to him. This is a customized approach and is more involved, perhaps going beyond what most would consider "ordinary Catholic" effort. Only you can decide if the possible payoff justifies the investment.

'NOT NOW" – CUSTOM APPROACH

In short, this custom approach requires us to (a) know what issues he considers important, (b) have information that connects those issues to the Church or the Catholic faith, and (c) recognize the best opportunities to share nuggets of information with Johnny that will seed his interest. This is not an easy approach, mostly because it requires us to develop our own understanding of certain subjects before we are prepared for action.

In normal times we would need to probe to figure out which issues are on Johnny's mind, what is relevant to him. But these are not normal times.

TODAY'S OPPORTUNITY

Try declaring in a small circle at your next cocktail party that the world has gone insane. You will not get much pushback. More likely everyone will chime in with supporting evidence. Cities burning. Statues torn down. Hong Kong besieged. Virus spreading. Hate everywhere. Schools and churches closed. Fake news. The list goes on – you'll need another round or two of drinks.

Johnny isn't oblivious to what's going on the world. He hears about it, thinks about it, tries to make sense of it. We know it is *relevant* to him. This spells *opportunity* for us if we can (a) discover for ourselves the connection between the current insanity in the world and the Catholic Church (past and present), and (b) intrigue Johnny about the connection by passing nuggets of information his way.

JOHNNY'S VIEW OF THE CHURCH

We assume that Johnny knows very little about the Catholic Church today, and that what he has heard lately is probably negative, such as sex scandals, financial scandals, church and school consolidations, etc.

And we assume he knows virtually nothing of the Church's history over the last fifty years. (Of course by now, you do know pretty much – your ace in the hole.)

Conclusion: Johnny does not know that society's insanity and chaos is matched by (and related to) insanity and chaos in the Catholic Church. Moreover, he cannot see how events in society over the last fifty years overlay and relate to events in the Church over that same period. When he begins to see this, he will be well on his way to resolving blind spots he may have today in recognizing risks in his behaviors and beliefs.

THE ANTI-CHURCH

The linchpin connecting society and Church is the anti-Church. What is it? It is the "counter-Church" that we have long been told will be created and used by Satan in his battle to overthrow Christ's Church. Wait! Before you declare me nuts, know that I am not inventing the term anti-Church. Nor am I dreaming up the very real war it is having with Christ's True Church. But I would not expect you to take my word for it, as it does sound incredible.[127] Take St. John Paul II's word for it, back in 1976:

---

[127] I am just an ordinary Catholic, and not so long ago was skeptical about this sort of thing ... as you may be right now.

"We are now standing in the face of the greatest historical confrontation humanity has gone through. I do not think that wide circles of American society or wide circles of the Christian community realize this fully. We are now facing the final confrontation between the Church and the anti-Church, of the Gospel versus the anti-Gospel.[128]

Father Linus Clovis, in a 2017 speech given in Rome, gave the following introduction prior to citing many specifics and implications of the anti-Church:

A hidden conflict has been raging in the Church for over one hundred years: a conflict explicitly revealed to Pope Leo XIII, partially contained by St. Pius X, unleashed at Vatican II ... Though he unmasked Modernism, [Pius X] failed to uproot it and, like the cockle in the field, it continued growing and developing ideals, doctrines and goals that were quite alien, if not diametrically opposed to the Catholic Church. Thus, Modernism, remaining within the Catholic Church, has metastasized into the anti-Church.

UNDERSTANDING THE ANTI-CHURCH

If you want to get Johnny's attention, even though he has a "Not now" attitude, you will need to know a lot about the anti-Church. An in-depth explanation is too extensive for this book, so a bit more information is provided in the Appendix, along with referrals to more qualified sources for the scholarly case (looking at history going back centuries, especially the last 100 years). In the meantime, just know that a basic understanding of the anti-Church (past and present) requires familiarity with many of the following events and movements:

- Pope Leo XIII's 1884 vision. *"According to Pope Leo XIII the Lord reminded Satan that his Church was imperishable. Satan then replied, "Grant me one century and more power of those who will serve me,*

---

128 Cardinal Karol Wojtyla, 1976 speech given in the United States, reprinted in The Wall Street Journal, November 9, 1978 shortly after he became Pope John Paul II.

and I will destroy it." Our Lord granted him 100 years. The Lord then revealed the events of the 20th century to Leo XIII. He saw wars, immorality, genocide and apostasy on a large scale.[129]

- The six appearances of Our Lady at Fatima in 1917[130], and the three secrets given to Lucia:

    1. *Vision of Hell*

    2. *World Wars I and II, Warning that if man continues offending God and Russia is not consecrated to the Immaculate Heart of Mary – The evils of Russia will spread about the world.*

    3. *An "apocalyptic" scene involving a pope and much carnage (though the Church's disclosure of the third secret has met with considerable controversy)*

- Marian apparitions at Quito, Chile (late 1500's), and recently at Akita and Civitavecchia

- The intrusive histories of:

    - Communism

    - Freemasonry

    - Artificial contraception and abortion

    - Cultural movements such as feminism and gay rights

    - Modernism in society

    - Modernism in the Catholic Church

    - Systems of thought such as Materialism, Rationalism, and Moral Relativism

---

129 Catholic News Agency, February 1, 2013

130 Just FYI … If I were to recommend to any Catholic one place to start brushing up on the Church and the Faith, it would be the story of Fatima. It opens many avenues of interest for research. And it ensures an introduction to the most astounding, foreseen, and documented miracle in modern times – the Miracle of the Sun.

I cannot stress enough how important understanding the anti-Church is in enabling the ordinary Catholic to understand our current times. A "layperson's" grasp of the anti-Church was possibly the greatest gift from those years at Mom's kitchen table.

But how do we use it to break through with Johnny?

EXPLANATORY POWER OF THE ANTI-CHURCH

A basic understanding of the anti-Church enables us to connect what is happening in today's society with the Church's present and past, which is critical in grabbing Johnny's attention. Conversation with him always starts with current events because, frankly, those are what preoccupy his mind. It is surprising how many topic areas can be fertile ground: from global warming to transgenderism to socialism.

NUGGETS FOR JOHNNY

Our goal is to share with him, when opportunity presents, nuggets of information tying these current events back to the Church or the Catholic faith. Nuggets are thought-starters, most effective when they are provocative or improbable-sounding, but they do not need to be. They do, however, need to be true - always. Trust that if nuggets are *intriguing* enough, discussion and investigation will eventually flow. Note: the anti-Church, while sobering, is very *intriguing* - especially when one can point out what was foreseen decades ago, even centuries ago, and is so clearly transpiring today.

Below are some example nuggets.

Topic	Nugget … "Did you know that …"
Aggression by China, such as: • Crack down on Hong Kong • Origination of Covid 19	• The Vatican has a "deal" with China, giving the communist government say in who gets to be a bishop? • There are two Catholic churches in China, one underground (loyal to the Pope), the other approved by the communist government? • In 1917, Mary gave a secret to three children, foretelling that communism would wreak havoc around the globe?
Rioting and Protesting in U.S. cities: • Racial equality • City leadership	• Catholic churches are being burned and vandalized around the country? • A well-known U.S. bishop proclaimed that defending religious statues in public spaces is laity's responsibility? • 70 years ago, Archbishop Sheen warned us that the anti-Christ would *make men shrink in shame if their fellowmen say they are not broadminded and liberal*
Covid 19 developments: • Local • National	• The U.S. bishops aren't even complaining that churches are closed by government order? • Some priestly societies will only distribute communion on-the-tongue, even in Covid times? • Many Catholic dioceses have imposed stricter Covid rules than required by civil authorities?

Domestic Politics, such as: • Green Deal / Democratic Socialism • LGBTQ rights	• Way back in the 1940's Archbishop Sheen told us all this was coming, even the "cancel culture"? • Two Archbishops (Vigano and Gregory) openly fought over President Trump's behavior and politics in Washington DC? • The Church is well on its way to approving same-sex marriages? • Artificial contraception was a precursor to the homosexual agenda?
Global Politics, such as: • U.N. Sustainable Development Goals • Nationalism and borders	• The Vatican hosts summits to promote the UN's SDG, and invites people like Jeffrey Sachs (population control advocate) to speak? • The U.S. Conference of Catholic Bishops receives hundreds of millions of dollars from the U.S. Government to assist in immigration services? (and the USCCB is vocally pro-immigration)

You do not have to jump into debate over these topics with him, nor do you really want to. Toss it out there and suggest that if he wonders about it, he should check it out. The "did you know …" method of interjecting an idea is non-confrontational and is usually received in a spirit of sharing. Do not shy away from topics that may seem to reflect badly on the Catholic Church … these may lead Johnny to recognize signs of the anti-Church![131] Feel sure that if he does investigate a topic or discuss one with you, he is getting out of the starting blocks … first steps toward him seeing for himself more relevance in the Catholic faith.

---

131   Many, many roads of research lead back to the anti-Church. Be ready to discuss it. Feel free to dare Johnny to Google the anti-Church, but probably not until you have gotten a bit down the road with him.

Be on the lookout, over time, for signals to spring into action as outlined in the "Tell me more" section above! And of course, never lose faith in the basic actions we lean on when our child is more like "Talk to the hand."

ONWARD. PROPELLED BY TRADITION

By now I hope you have a new fervor for helping Johnny get to a place where he recognizes the risks he may be taking in getting to heaven. While organizing your thoughts, here are a few to keep in mind.

NO FAULT

No matter where and when we try to help our children engage more in their faith, there is a chance they will feel preached to, or accused of failing somehow. No one takes kindly to either. But does this need to happen? Maybe not: if we can adopt a new overarching attitude ourselves. Combining our knowledge of the Ember stories and the anti-Church, we see Johnny's situation in a new light. We can actually understand why he has not been excited about Catholicism, why he said "I don't get anything out of Mass," why he finds Church positions on important social issues so wrong or confusing, and so much else. As it turns out, our kids are pretty perceptive. The "problems" have been real, their doubts and questions and disinterest aren't all that irrational. But here is our new point of view: our children are not at fault. Do not be afraid to tell them that. Freely assume the burden of guilt. Affirm that many of the Church's teachings do not seem logical because background (some of which they were denied) is necessary to understand the logic. Make sure they know that others have no intention of being judgmental. In fact, tell them their fellow Catholics hope they will give the true Church a chance to right the injustices done to them. The greatest injustice has been depriving them of Catholic Tradition, which as we've seen, deprived them of the full Deposit of the Faith. Rectifying this will not be easy, but the Church stands ready when Johnny is.

EYE ON THE BALL

As we proceed, we need to keep our eye on the ball, and steer Johnny's eyes the same direction. Here is the simplest picture I can imagine for the purpose:

Today, and for the rest of his life, Johnny (presently in the middle) is being pulled right and pulled left, by opposing forces. Those two forces, the Church and Anti-Church, are at war. The Church lays out the Deposit of the Faith, and the anti-Church tempts Johnny to take risks. If, or when, it seems difficult to distinguish between the two, resort to Matthew's rule of thumb (9:16): judge everything by its fruits. The anti-Church's fruits are:

- Society awash in divorce, violence, human trafficking, pornography, abortion, multi-genderism, same-sex marriage, fatherlessness, greed, and on and on.

- A Roman Catholic Church unmoored from Tradition, in tatters (by every measure imaginable), and unable or unwilling to resist society's march toward darkness.

It is never difficult to unmask the anti-Church, if we stay on watch.

POWER OF THE TRADITIONAL LATIN MASS

It may have seemed that the Ember stories placed an inordinate emphasis on the Traditional Latin Mass (TLM). The TLM is, after all, not the whole of Catholic Tradition. But it is a very important, powerful part of it. The progressive bishops at Vatican II knew this and made the Mass a central target from the beginning of the Council. What about the TLM made it such a high-priority target for them?

> *"The Latin Mass takes the mysteries seriously. It is like dealing with eternal mysteries in a serious, convicted way ... I want*

*to go to a Mass that is bigger than me, that is challenging ...
I get to pray at the Mass. I get to meditate at the Mass!"...
The TLM does a great job of forming [my young children]...
They are aware that something important is happening, even
if they don't know what that thing is ... beautiful art, this
profound music you don't hear anywhere else, these things
signal to them that something important is happening."* [132]
Cameron O'Hearn

*"The traditional Latin Mass is the Mass of all ages because of the
fact that its rite expresses in a clearer and more beautiful manner
the essential truth of the sacrifice of Mass, i.e., the adoration of
God the Father, which Jesus Christ, His Incarnate Son, offered
on the Cross in the name of the whole of creation in the power of
the Holy Spirit. .... Young people feel in the depths of their souls
that they are born for a higher ideal, even for heroism. The style
of the Novus Ordo Mass, with its significantly reduced sacredness and ritual beauty, instead transmits mediocrity ... the traditional Latin Mass has increasingly become the Mass of youth."* [133]
Bishop Athanasius Schneider

*"How does the blue collar worker (who might be too busy to read
a book by Tim Staples) receive catechesis on the sacraments? The
answer is that for thousands of years, the catechesis happened
by kneeling at Holy Mass ... I mean that the serious Catholic
learned and prayed during the week as best he could. Then on
Sunday, everything he learned or offered was forged in a mys-
terious and powerful ritual that incorporated all his senses, his
intellect, his will ... if not a sign of the majesty of God, if not a
sign of the chasm between Creator and creature, this ritual was*

---

132 Cameron O'Hearn, Director/"Mass of the Ages" during interview "Latin Mass Goes mainstream, But Why?", Dr. Taylor Marshall, July 2020.

133 Christus Vincit by Bishop Athanasius Schneider in conversation with Diane Montagna, 2019.

simply too weird for a non-Catholic to approach ... the Traditional Latin Mass engenders catechesis because it engenders automatic reverence and intimacy ... the average illiterate Catholic learned that Jesus was truly present by simply attending Mass"[134]
Father David Nix

The Latin Mass is Sacred Tradition's beating heart. We will not have made a serious attempt to right the wrong done to Johnny (depriving him of Tradition), until introducing him to the Traditional Latin Mass.

TRADITION ON THE MOVE

Tradition is making a comeback among Catholics, notably with young Catholics. That is not to say that being a tradition-minded Catholic is cool. It is not supposed to be.[135] Still, Tradition and the TLM gaining in popularity probably improves the odds of Johnny taking it seriously. Be familiar with the status of Tradition's resurgence, especially the TLM, in your diocese or geographic region and make sure Johnny knows about it.

And from the Ember stories, other information to remember about the traditional brushfire crossing the land:

• How difficult it was to keep the flame of Tradition alive. Those before us earned the title Embers, and their stories can inspire today's Catholics and help us appreciate what we have.

• Tradition is not scary. There is nothing "new" about it, and its resurgence isn't a sudden phenomenon.

• Traditional Latin Masses are popping up (almost) everywhere, though it can vary greatly by diocese.

---

134 Father David Nix, Padre Peregrino "The over-intellectualization of the Catholic faith", *June 27, 2017*

135 Jesus was clear from the beginning, "because you are not of the world, but I have chosen you out of the world, therefore the world hates you ... if they have persecuted me, they will persecute you also." (John 15: 18-20)

- Clergy are still key. Heroic priests show up when the Church needs them, and have an impact on the challenges of the times, in both Church and society.

TIME AND TIMING

We know intuitively that the mission to help Johnny is a race against time. We may not want to think about it, but time could run out suddenly for any of us, including Johnny. That simple thought may motivate us and it may motivate Johnny. On the other hand, some of us are prone to procrastination, especially without a fixed deadline.

For added motivation, we need only realize that we are living at a moment of uniquely good timing to help Johnny, but also one that may not last long.

With respect to our mission with Johnny (and *only* in that respect), it is hard to imagine better conditions than those that exist right now. For over fifty years the anti-Church has operated stealthily, sowing confusion and smothering Catholic Tradition. This produced generations of Catholics who were much more easily lured into dangerous risk-taking in their behaviors and beliefs. The anti-Church's success is evidenced by the cultural decay in our society, which is apparent to all.

But during the decades of stealth activity it was difficult to detect the hand of the Church (or shall we say the anti-Church) in influencing society and culture. That has changed in the last ten years. Now, the insanity and chaos within the Catholic Church itself is bringing the anti-Church out into clear view for anyone who is looking. Red flags have been everywhere, for instance:

- Cardinal McCarrick, and Rome's opaque handling
- Pachamama statues in St. Peter's Cathedral
- Vatican Bank scandals

- Vatican promotion of the One World Order, including its climate change agenda

- The Abu Dhabi document and the Abrahamic Worship Center

- Archbishop Vigano's testimony

- Unceasing sex scandal among the U.S. and international clergy

- The Vatican's secret deal with China

- Fr. James Martin and the Church's bridge to LGBTQ

- Purging of conservatives from posts of authority in the Church

- Proliferation of progressive bishops in the United States

- Amoris Laetitia and the Dubia

- German synodal path

- Etc.

The list goes on, and details would fill volumes. Are you, the reader, familiar with most or all of these? If not, I hope you will Google them and encourage others to research them also. In Johnny's case, help him look. When he does, he will see the anti-Church exposed in clearer view than ever. This is the gift of our time … if we seize on it.

But, as mentioned, this current "good timing" may just be a window in time. We know from countless sources that as the anti-Church progresses the world approaches a huge, ugly, final conflict.[136] We obviously do not know when that will happen. But, at the same time, it is possible that "things" will continue to get uglier. A more fearful thought is that the ugliness continues to grow at an *increasing* rate, as it has over the most recent decade. If that be the case, confusion will continue to heighten. Souls may move quickly toward the anti-Church, some to rigid positions. And what can be seen as

---

136   Among the foreshadowings of the impending conflict is the message of Our Lady at Fatima, relayed by Lucia to Father Carlo Caffarra, *"a time will come when the decisive battle between the kingdom of Christ and Satan will be over marriage and the family."* Shortly before his death in 2017, then-Cardinal Caffarra stated, *"What Sister Lucia wrote to me is being fulfilled today".* That should be sobering for anyone alert to developments in our society and culture over the past fifty years.

"good timing" right now, might yield to a time where it is even harder to get through to Johnny.

Take action today, and make your family reunion in heaven an eventual reality.

And keep in mind … Our Blessed Mother knows the joy of being with her son for eternity. She will most certainly help, if you ask.

APPENDIX:
WHY THE CHURCH EXILED TRADITION

Smothering of Sacred Tradition over the past fifty years has been the work of the anti-Church in its battle with the Church. The following picture is used in Chapter Nine to depict the ongoing struggle between these two opposing forces:

I am not inventing the terms Church and Anti-Church, or the idea that the two are at war. St. John Paul II is one of many who have made this reference in modern times. In 1976, he (at the time Cardinal Karol Wojtyla) said in a speech in the United States:

> *We are now standing in the face of the greatest historical confrontation humanity has gone through. I do not think that wide circles of American society or wide circles of the Christian community realize this fully. We are now facing the final confrontation between the Church and the anti-Church, of the Gospel versus the anti-Gospel.*

THE ANTI CHURCH

Scholars have written extensively about the reality and effects of the anti-Christ and his anti-Church. Excellent examples include:

Christus Vincit[137] by Bishop Athanasius Schneider

The Anti-Church Has Come, But Don't Be Afraid[138] by Fr. Linus Clovis

Infiltration[139] by Dr. Taylor Marshall

Should ordinary Catholics be expected to inform themselves about the anti-Church? I say yes, but I realize this sounds like a stretch for most Catholics. I do believe that Catholics today (because of the very unique time in which we live) need to take a look at the concept of the anti-church, at least enough to form an opinion of it. The existence and actions of the anti-Church seem to explain an incredible amount of the inexplicable insanity and chaos that we see in both the Church and in society today (which makes it very valuable in our efforts with Johnny). For those who are not at all familiar with the anti-Church, the following writings from solid sources can serve as an introduction:

The Venerable Archbishop Fulton Sheen[140] warned of the anti-Christ and the anti-Church in his 1947 presentation titled "Signs of Our Times". Some excerpts:

From now on the struggle will be not for the colonies and national rights, but for the souls of men.

---

137 Christus Vincit, Christ's Triumph, by Bishop Athanasius Schneider and Diane Montagna, copyright 2019, Angelico Press

138 Address by Fr. Linus Clovis, spiritual director to Family Life International, May 18, 2017 at the fourth annual Rome Life Forum. https://voiceofthefamily.com/the-catholic-church-and-the-anti-church-currently-co-exist-in-the-same-sacramental-liturgical-and-juridical-space/

139 Infiltration, The Plot To Destroy The Church From Within, by Taylor R. Marshall, copyright 2019, Sophia Institute Press

140 Archbishop Sheen (1895-1979) was a respected teacher and gifted speaker. He hosted a radio program, The Catholic Hour for 22 years, reaching an estimated four million listeners at the height of its popularity. Then during his term as auxiliary bishop of New York he hosted a weekly television series, *Life Is Worth Living* (1951–57) that attracted about 30 million viewers.

[The anti-Christ] will set up a counter-Church which will be the ape of the Church because, he the devil, is the ape of God. It will have all the notes and characteristics of the Church, but in reverse and emptied of its divine content. It will be a mystical body of the anti-Christ that will in all externals resemble the mystical body of Christ.

The anti-Christ will not be so called, otherwise he would have no followers. He will wear no red tights, nor vomit sulphur, nor carry a trident nor wave an arrow tail as the Mephistophiles in Faust. This masquerade has helped the devil convince men that he does not exist, for he knows that he is never so strong as when men believe that he does not exist.

How will he come in this new age to win followers to his religion? He will come disguised as the Great Humanitarian; he will talk peace, prosperity and plenty not as means to lead us to God, but as ends in themselves; He will write books on the new idea of God to suit the way people live; induce faith in astrology so as to make not the will but the stars responsible for sins; he will explain Guilt away psychologically as inhibited eroticism, make men shrink in shame if their fellowmen say they are not broadminded and liberal; he will be so broadminded as to identify tolerance with indifference to right and wrong, truth and error; he will spread the lie that men will never be better until they make society better and thus have selfishness to provide fuel for the next revolution; he will foster science but only to have armament makers use one marvel of science to destroy another; he will foster more divorces under the disguise that another partner is "vital"; he will increase love for love and decrease love for person; he will invoke religion to destroy religion; he will even speak of Christ and say that he was the greatest man who ever lived; his mission he will say will be to liberate men from the servitudes of superstition and Fascism: which he will never define; he will organize children's games, tell people who they should and should not marry and unmarry, who should bear children and who should not; he will benevolently draw chocolate bars from his pockets for the little ones and bottles of milk for the Hottentots ... He wants no proclamation of immutable principles from the lofty heights of a Church, but mass organization through propaganda where only a common man directs the idiosyncracies of common men. Opinions not truths, commentators not teachers, Gallup polls not principles, nature not grace - and to these golden calves will men toss themselves from their Christ.

There are many current Catholic experts essentially aligned with Archbishop Sheen on the subject.

Father Dwight Longenecker reflected in 2018 on Archbishop Sheen's still "strong and sobering" vision of the Anti-Church and implored today's Catholics to pay attention:

Catholics need to wake up. Already most of us have adapted to the Spirit of the new age. Already we have compromised our standards and lowered our defenses. It has been a slow, gradual process, but why do we think that we might stand up to the antichrist when we have already swallowed his candy?

Look at the world around you. How many church leaders do you know who already preach a gospel that is no more than watered down socialism? How many sweet talking, smiling preachers do you already know who parade their political activism while neglecting the reality of Christ's true gospel? How many religious people do you know who already believe that it is all about the brotherhood of Man while neglecting the Fatherhood of God?

At this time there is no single false prophet or counterfeit church. Instead these false systems of thought have infiltrated all the Christian churches and the Catholic church is no exception. When I hear prelates talk more about saving the environment than saving souls I'm smelling sulphur. When I hear priests and prelates justifying a sexual immorality that breaks the sacrament of marriage and the natural order in the cause of "peace and mercy" I'm smelling smoke–and it ain't incense. When I hear prelates compromise the Catholic faith in favor of a false ecumenism I'm whiffing something vile from the sewers of Dis.

Already they have put before us "a new religion without a Cross, a liturgy without a world to come, a religion to destroy a religion, or a politics which is a religion–one that renders unto Caesar even the things that are God's."

Father Linus Clovis' 2017 speech, given in Rome, was cited in Chapter 9. Several additional thoughts from that speech:

It is self-evident that the Catholic Church and the anti-Church currently co-exist in the same sacramental, liturgical and juridical space. The latter, having grown stronger, is now attempting to pass itself off as the true Church, all the better to induct, or coerce, the faithful into becoming adherents, promoters and defenders of a secular ideology.

To achieve its objectives, the anti-Church, in collaboration with the secular powers, uses the law and media to browbeat the true Church into submission. By adroit use of the media, the activists of the anti-Church have managed to intimidate bishops, clergy and most of the Catholic press into silence. Equally, the lay faithful are terrorized by fear of the hostility, ridicule and hate that would be visited upon them should they object to the imposition of LGBT ideology.

The blood-dimmed tide is loosed as there emerges from the darkness and confusion a real and open conflict between those who remain faithful and loyal to Our Lord's Gospel and the increasing numbers of the *uncatechised, who, by adhering to the praxis of 'political correctness' formulated by LGBT ideologues, reject the Christian Gospel. The open and unilateral imposition of this politically correct ideology in many parishes and dioceses is validating an anti-Church that is in opposition to the Catholic Church, the true Church of Christ.*

Christ, however, does warn us about the soul killers, namely, the *"many false prophets (who) will arise and lead many astray"*, especially those prophets who *"show signs and wonders, to lead astray, if possible, the elect."* Further, since the world will speak approvingly of these false prophets, they will be readily believed by people who *"will not endure sound teaching, but having itching ears they will accumulate for themselves teachers to suit their own likings, and will turn away from listening to the truth and wander into myths"*.

These lengthy excerpts have been included because the anti-Church is a very important tool in understanding the last fifty years and the overlap of Church and society. It is the kind of concept that Johnny may be interested in, and it could be key in helping Johnny figure out the big picture for himself.

EXAMPLES ABOUND

Signs and warnings of the anti-Church abound today. The vast majority of normal Catholics may not even be aware of these. They should be, though, and for those who will take the time to familiarize themselves, the anti-Church will come into clearer focus. At the very least, these are fascinating studies … the kind that Johnny may eventually find interesting, even enlightening.

DUMPSTER FIRE IN D.C.

Washington D.C., Jun 2, 2020 / 10:10 am MT (CNA)

Amid burgeoning conflict regarding the president's response to riots across the country, President Donald Trump visited the Saint John Paul II National Shrine in Washington, D.C.

Washington D.C., Jun 2, 2020 / 10:10 am MT (CNA)

Archbishop Wilton Gregory of Washington, D.C. said on Tuesday morning: "I find it baffling and reprehensible that any Catholic facility would allow itself to be so egregiously misused and manipulated in a fashion that violates our religious principles, which call us to defend the rights of all people even those with whom we might disagree."

June 3, 2020 open letter Archbishop Carlo Maria Vigano (former Apostolic Nuncio to the United States of America) to priests and laity of the archdiocese of Washington.

Over the past twenty years, your [archdiocese] of Washington, in particular and now for the third time, has been and continues to be deeply afflicted and wounded by false shepherds whose way of life is full of lies, deceits, lust and corruption. Wherever they have been, they were a cause of serious scandal for various local Churches, for your entire country and for the whole Church... "Do not follow them, as they lead you to perdition. They are mercenaries. They teach and practice falsehoods and corruption! ... Follow with perseverance the teachings and examples of the holy pastors and priests who are among you.

June 7, 2020 letter to Donald Trump from Archbishop Carlo Maria Vigano

Mr. President, In recent months we have been witnessing the formation of two opposing sides that I would call Biblical: the children of light and the children of darkness ... In society, Mr. President, these two opposing realities co-exist as eternal enemies, just as God and

*Satan are eternal enemies ... There are faithful Shepherds who care
for the flock of Christ, but there are also mercenary infidels who
seek to scatter the flock and hand the sheep over to be devoured by
ravenous wolves. ... For the first time, the United States has in you
a President who courageously defends the right to life, who is not
ashamed to denounce the persecution of Christians throughout the
world, who speaks of Jesus Christ and the right of citizens to freedom
of worship ... I dare to believe that both of us are on the same side
in this battle, albeit with different weapons.*

All this within one week, and probably not even noticed by the vast majority
of Catholics in the United States! Yet, just like so many other developments
in our society and Church these days, the influence (and warning signs) of
the anti-Church are there:

- Conflict between bishops ... as foretold by the Blessed Virgin Mary
  at Fatima.

- False Shepherds, full of lies, deceits, lust and corruption ... as
  anticipated by virtually all of those who have described the coming anti-Church

- An Archbishop (Gregory) portraying the President as one who does
  not "defend the rights of all people even those with whom we might
  disagree"... as Archbishop Sheen predicted ("make men shrink in
  shame if their fellowmen say they are not broadminded and liberal;
  he will be so broadminded as to identify tolerance with indifference
  to right and wrong, truth and error")

- An Archbishop (Vigano) reaching out to a public official to alert
  him to the anti-Church, and to encourage him to fight against it in
  his realm of influence.

One might ask why an archbishop would reprimand a Catholic shrine for
allowing a United States President and First Lady to pay honor to our Lord.
If the reader is not familiar with the last three Archbishops of Washington

D.C. (those called false shepherds by Archbishop Vigano), I beg you do a little research. The current Archbishop of DC is Wilton Gregory and he was preceded by Donald Wuerl, who was preceded by Theodore McCarrick. I hope Theodore McCarrick is a familiar name (he was de-frocked in 2019 due to his years of disgraceful abuse of children.) Wilton Gregory, who is just now settling in as DC Archbishop, was the Bishop of Belleville Illinois from 1993-2004, a period during which he smothered Tradition (as we learned in the Ember stories), and also served as President of the United States Council of Catholic Bishops (USCCB).

CHINA AND THE CATHOLIC CHURCH

National Catholic Reporter September 24, 2018 The Vatican's deal with China

Finally, the Vatican has done a deal with China, or rather with the ruling Chinese Communist Party that has been conducting an escalating program of repression against religion. The deal is already drenched in controversy and opposed by many Chinese Catholics and anti-pope conservatives ... the regularization of bishops' appointments was always the central goal of these talks that have taken five years to bear any fruit ... For its part, the Vatican has officially recognized eight bishops previously not recognized by Rome and/or previously excommunicated. One of those bishops died in 2017 ... This is one of the key points of the deal that has angered leaders of China's so-called underground Catholics, leaders who have refused to join the Communist Party-controlled Catholic Patriotic Association. Various estimates, including by the U.S. government, say underground Catholics make up as much as 50 percent of the country's estimated 10 million -12 million Catholics ... Leaked information of the deal triggered a resistance movement whose case had been publicly and aggressively prosecuted by Hong Kong's politically active retired bishop, Cardinal Joseph Zen Ze-kiun, 86, who was born in

Shanghai. "They're giving the flock into the mouths of the wolves. It's an incredible betrayal".

Almost two years later, the Vatican's "deal" with the Chinese Communist Party (CCP) is still a closely-guarded secret. Even Bishops from China are not privy to the details. Developments in the country since the deal was signed are clearly not positive, at least with regard to faithful Catholics and their right to worship freely. I encourage the reader to seek out further details – they are not hard to find. For our purposes, focus should be on the simple fact that Rome is flirting with China, an aggressive Communist power. There is no question that Communism and its principles are the "evils of Russia" that our Lady of Fatima warned would be spread around the world. China is the most active vehicle for their spread these days. Yet the Catholic faith is incompatible with these evils, co-existence is not possible. At the very least, the Vatican is playing with fire. At worst, anti-Church forces are aligning in some way with forces that are extremely opposed to fundamental Catholic beliefs. Sadly, it appears that faithful Catholics in China are being increasingly persecuted. Facts such as the secrecy of the deal, and stiff-arming by Rome of any "opposition" to the Vatican-China deal add fuel to prospects that we are seeing another manifestation of the anti-Church.

"THE DUBIA", 2015

Formal effort by four Cardinals to get clarification from the Pope regarding doctrinally-questionable statements in an official Papal document, Amoris Laetitia. Years have passed with no response, and no attempt at explanation from the Vatican.

[Key Takeaway: false or misleading teaching that will not be defined ... to be expected in the anti-Church]

ABU DHABI DOCUMENT, 2019 /
ABRAHAMIC FAMILY HOUSE, 2020

On Februrary 4, 2019, Pope Francis signed the "Document on Human Fraternity for World Peace and Living Together" with Grand Imam Ahmad el-Tayeb in Abu Dhabi. The document has been particularly controversial for a passage stating that God wills the diversity of religions. Numerous Church officials have called for clarification and even deletion of the statement. None has been given by the Pope.

Following from the Abu Dhabi statement has come the planned Abrahamic Family House, an interfaith complex in Abu Dhabi that will contain a church, mosque and synagogue. The designer expressed his motivation, "to encourage "peaceful co-existence and acceptance" of the three Abrahamic faiths Christianity, Islam and Judaism in the UAE's capital city."

[Key Takeaway: False Ecumenism ... to be expected in the anti-Church]

AMAZONIAN SYNOD / PACHAMAMA

In late 2019, perhaps the most well-known of the recent "synods" organized by the Vatican. Several highly-controversial initiatives were promoted and may be implemented in the follow-on. Pachamama statues, prominent in several locations at the synod, were highly controversial. To many onlookers the statues symbolize pagan idolatry. The Vatican has yet to disprove that assertion or to provide any other meaningful explanation.

[Key Takeaway: False idolatry ... to be expected in the anti-Church]

RACE TO NORMALIZE SEXUAL AND GENDER CONFUSION

Most breathing humans in the U.S. are familiar with the push for wide-spread acceptance of every sort of sexual attraction and gender identity imaginable. Sex and gender confusion are extensive subjects, but the movement (which is tied to the artificial contraception and abortion movements) is bringing to life one very troubling prophesy … In the 1980's Sister Lucia (the girl to whom the Blessed Virgin spoke at Fatima) wrote a message she had received from Our Lady, "a time will come when the decisive battle between the kingdom of Christ and Satan will be over marriage and the family". Pope St. Paul VI also noted the dangers in *Humanae Vitae.*

[Key Takeaway: the nuclear (traditional) family being destroyed … to be expected in the times of the anti-Church]

PHOTO AND IMAGE CREDITS

1. *Panoramic View of St. Mary's Church, School, Convent, and Rectory, 1943: Program / 50 Years in Retrospective, History of St. Mary's Parish*

2. *Belleville Square: Courtesy of Belleville Historical Society / belleville-historicalsociety.org*

3. *St. Mary's Church Altar, 1970: Courtesy of Mary Wenzel*

4. *Interior of St. Mary's Church, 1993: St. Mary's Church Directory / Olan Mills studios*

5. *Exterior of Immaculate Conception Church: Augustinas Žemaitis, http://global.truelithuania.com ,Google street view*

6. *Interior of Immaculate Conception Church: Augustinas Žemaitis, http://global.truelithuania.com*

7. *Exterior of Clara Hempelmann building: Toby Weiss / beltstl.com*

8. *Doors at Clara Hempelmann building: Toby Weiss / beltstl.com*

9. *Mass in Basement of Clara Hempelmann building: Courtesy of Peggy Meuhlemann*

10. *Photo of Log Church, Cahokia IL: Historic Village of Cahokia website / Google Maps photo*

11. *Location of Log Church graphic: R.J. Wenzel*